Julia Hümmer

Landeskunde kreativ: ABC of the USA

Arbeitsblätter für den Englischunterricht
Klasse 7–9

Verlag an der Ruhr

Impressum

Titel
Landeskunde kreativ: ABC of the USA
Arbeitsblätter für den Englischunterricht – Klasse 7–9

Autorin
Julia Hümmer

Umschlagmotive
Landkarte © TALVA – Shutterstock.com,
Freiheitsstatue © Yanina Nosova – Shutterstock.com

Sensitivity Reading
Anna Lena Lutz (S. 14, 15, 22, 23, 53, 68–75)

Satz und Layout
Reemers Publishing Service, Thomas Krauß

Druck
Heenemann GmbH & Co. KG, Berlin, DE

Verlag an der Ruhr
Mülheim an der Ruhr
www.verlagruhr.de

Geeignet für die Klassen 7–9

Urheberrechtlicher Hinweis
Das Werk und seine Teile sind urheberrechtlich geschützt. Jede Verwendung in anderen als den gesetzlich zugelassenen Fällen oder außerhalb dieser Bedingungen bedarf der vorherigen schriftlichen Einwilligung des Verlages. Im Werk vorhandene Kopiervorlagen dürfen vervielfältigt werden, allerdings nur für Schüler*innen der eigenen Klasse/des eigenen Kurses. Die dazu notwendigen Informationen (Buchtitel, Verlag und Autorin) haben wir für Sie als Service bereits mit eingedruckt. Diese Angaben dürfen weder verändert noch entfernt werden. Die Weitergabe von Kopiervorlagen oder Kopien (auch von Ihnen veränderte) an Kolleg*innen, Eltern oder Schüler*innen anderer Klassen/Kurse ist nicht gestattet. Der Verlag untersagt ausdrücklich das Herstellen von digitalen Kopien, das digitale Speichern und Zurverfügungstellen dieser Materialien in Netzwerken (das gilt auch für Intranets von Schulen und sonstigen Bildungseinrichtungen), per E-Mail, Internet oder sonstigen elektronischen Medien außerhalb der gesetzlichen Grenzen. Kein Verleih. Keine gewerbliche Nutzung.
Näheres zu unseren Lizenzbedingungen können Sie unter www.verlagruhr.de/lizenzbedingungen/ nachlesen.

Bitte beachten Sie zusätzlich die Informationen unter www.schulbuchkopie.de.

Soweit in diesem Produkt Personen fotografisch abgebildet sind und ihnen von der Redaktion fiktive Namen, Berufe, Dialoge u. Ä. zugeordnet oder diese Personen in bestimmte Kontexte gesetzt werden, dienen diese Zuordnungen und Darstellungen ausschließlich der Veranschaulichung und dem besseren Verständnis des Inhalts.

© Verlag an der Ruhr 2024
ISBN 978-3-8346-6497-6

PEFC zertifiziert
Dieses Produkt stammt aus nachhaltig bewirtschafteten Wäldern und kontrollierten Quellen.
www.pefc.de
PEFC/04-31-1156

Inhaltsverzeichnis

Vorwort 5

★ The USA – An Overview 7

What is this chapter about? 7
The United States of America 8
The Red, White and Blue 10
Mix it, baby! 12
The Northeast – Massachusetts 14
The Midwest – Indiana 16
The West – California 18
The South – Louisiana 20
More creativity 22

★ Cities and Sights 29

What is this chapter about? 29
New York City 30
Chicago 32
Los Angeles 35
Las Vegas 37
National parks 39
Niagara Falls 41
More creativity 43

★ From History to Stories 51

What is this chapter about? 51
Pocahontas and the early colonists 52
Sitting Bull: a fighter for his people 54
Education for extinction 56
Standing up at Standing Rock 58
George Washington and the American Revolution 60
From miners to millions: the story of Levi Strauss 62
Honest Abe's quest for unity 64
Harriet Tubman: a guiding light to freedom 66
"No." – How Rosa Parks took a stand for justice 68
Celebrating excellence: the Obamas' footprint 70

Inhaltsverzeichnis

Action for equality: Black Lives Matter ... 72
Roselle's remarkable rescue: guiding hope on 9/11 ... 74
More creativity ... 76

★ Culture Kaleidoscope ... 77

What is this chapter about? ... 77
Team spirit! ... 78
Let's celebrate! ... 80
High school stories ... 82
Harmonizing with the stars ... 84

★ Anhang ... 86

Reflexionsimpulse ... 86

★ Lösungen ... 88

The USA – Scavenger Hunt (S. 25–26) ... 88

Download

Ihr persönlicher Zugang:

Alle im Download enthaltenen Dateien können Sie unter folgendem Link oder über das Einscannen des QR-Codes herunterladen:

Passwort: Landeskunde*Reflexion
Sollten der Link und der QR-Code
ihre Gültigkeit verlieren,
wenden Sie sich bitte an
digitaleslernen@verlagruhr.de

QR Code is registered trademark of DENSO WAVE INCORPORATED

Vorwort

⭐ Die USA – das Land der unbegrenzten Möglichkeiten

Die USA sind für unsere Schüler*innen[1] nach wie vor ein Land, das ihnen oft nahesteht und über das sie bereits vermeintlich viel wissen. Durch Medien, Filme, Musik und auch die sozialen Medien rückt die Welt immer weiter in die Lebenswelt unserer Lernenden und so kommen sie oft schon mit einer ganz bestimmten Vorstellung über die USA in den Englischunterricht.

Doch nicht immer vermitteln die Kanäle, die unsere Schüler*innen konsumieren, ein differenziertes Bild und so verfestigen sich Vorurteile mehr und mehr. Dabei sind die USA viel mehr als ihre Stereotype: nämlich ein Land voller Geschichten und unbegrenzter Möglichkeiten, diese zu erzählen.

Weil dieses Heft jedoch nur begrenzt viel Platz bietet, erfolgte eine exemplarische Auswahl von Themen, die für Schüler*innen gleichermaßen motivierend wie auch herausfordernd wirken. Sie ermöglichen neue Blickwinkel, einen Einbezug der eigenen Lebenswelt und viele kreative Bearbeitungsmöglichkeiten. Bitte beachten Sie, dass das Heft hindurch immer wieder Ereignisse zur Sprache kommen, in deren Kontext Menschen Gewalt angetan wurde (z. B. Vertreibung, Diskriminierung oder physische Gewalt). Achten Sie daher bei der Auswahl der Themen für Ihren Unterricht auf sich und Ihre Lernenden.

⭐ „Völkerverständigung" – Ist das noch zeitgemäß?

Der Begriff „Völkerverständigung", wie er zum Beispiel in Art. 2 Abs. 1 Bayerisches Gesetz über das Erziehungs- und Unterrichtswesen erwähnt wird, kommt so verstaubt daher, dass er kaum noch verwendet wird. Und dabei ist er vielleicht wichtiger denn je: Plurale Gesellschaften, voneinander abhängige Wirtschaftssysteme, immer enger vernetzte internationale Beziehungen, politische Konflikte und Kriege brauchen gegenseitiges Verständnis, Wertschätzung und Respekt. In diesem Zusammenhang ist es nicht damit getan, oberflächliche Vorurteile zu wiederholen, sondern es ist genaues Hinsehen auf das gefordert, was uns alle am Ende verbindet.

⭐ BANI, 4K und Schule?

Wenn wir mal über den Tellerrand schauen, dann können wir aus anderen Disziplinen viel lernen und wichtige Impulse für unseren täglichen Einsatz in der Schule mitnehmen. Der US-amerikanische Zukunftsforscher Jamais Cascio beschrieb im Jahr 2020 unsere Welt erstmals als „BANI" – eine Welt, die sich als *brittle, anxious, non-linear* und *incomprehensible* verstehen lässt[2]. Eine Welt, in der Systeme spröde sind, brechen können, weil sie nicht so stark sind wie bisher angenommen. Eine Welt, die Angst fördert. Angst, die entsteht, weil man befürchtet, falsche Entscheidungen zu treffen, niemals richtigliegen zu können. Eine Welt, in der Kausalitäten nur noch bedingt gelten. Kleine Ursachen können massive Reaktionen auslösen, der Ausgang

---

[1] Der Verlag an der Ruhr legt großen Wert auf eine geschlechtergerechte und inklusive Sprache. Daher nutzen wir neutrale Formulierungen oder das Gendersternchen, um alle Menschen unabhängig von Geschlecht oder Geschlechtsidentität einzuschließen. In Texten für Schüler*innen finden sich aus didaktischen Gründen neutrale Begriffe bzw. Doppelformen.

[2] Vgl. Cascio, Jamais (29.04.2020): Facing the Age of Chaos, Link: https://medium.com/@cascio/facing-the-age-of-chaos-b00687b1f51d, zuletzt abgerufen am 14.05.2024.

Vorwort

einer Handlung ist mitunter nur schwer abzuschätzen. Eine Welt, die uns unverständlich ist, weil sie zu komplex ist oder wir Ursachen nicht mehr nachvollziehen können.

Die Welt, in der unsere Lernenden aufwachsen, ist BANI. Und sie wird es auch bleiben. Oder vielmehr: Wir haben keine Ahnung, wie genau die Welt aussehen wird, auf die wir Schüler*innen heute vorbereiten wollen. Wir müssen ihnen also nicht nur Wissen, sondern vor allem Kompetenzen an die Hand geben, die es ihnen ermöglichen, in einer BANI-Welt zurechtzukommen.

Nach dem 4K-Modell des Lernens geht es genau darum: Die vier wichtigsten Zukunftskompetenzen zu fördern, nämlich Kreativität, Kollaboration, kritisches Denken und Kommunikation.

Sollten diese Ansätze aus der Wirtschaft Einzug in die Schule halten? Gehören sie da wirklich hin? Ich meine ja. Mit genügend eigenem kritischen Denken können wir uns die *key takeaways* doch auch selbst suchen.

Ist das was für mich? Für meine Schüler*innen? Dieses Themenheft richtet sich an all die Lehrkräfte, die bereit sind, alte Pfade zu verlassen, ohne gleich das Rad neu erfinden zu wollen. Lehrkräfte, die ihren Schüler*innen ermöglichen wollen, *outside the box* zu denken und zu lernen, sind hier richtig.

★ Zum Einsatz dieses Heftes

An die Infotexte, die man beispielsweise klassisch mit Lesen im Unterricht oder im Sinne des *flipped classroom* vorbereitend bearbeiten lassen kann, schließen sich verschiedene Aufgabentypen an, die verschiedene Zugänge auf unterschiedlichen Lernniveaus und damit echte Differenzierung ermöglichen. Das Heft richtet sich vor allem an Lernende der Jahrgangsstufen 7 bis 9 und lässt sich durch die vielen offenen Aufgabenformen bunt durch die verschiedenen Schularten einsetzen.

Thematisch ergänzt das Heft die gängigen Lehrwerke. Die Themen sind in sich abgeschlossen, können also als eigene kurze Einheiten oder sogar als Vertretungsstunden eingesetzt werden. Darüber hinaus lassen sich die Materialien auch im Rahmen von Projekten gut zum Einsatz bringen.

Jedes Thema an sich lädt nach seiner kreativen Bearbeitung zu einer Reflexion ein: über die Inhalte, den Arbeitsverlauf, die Erkenntnisse oder auch die Ergebnisse. Mögliche Reflexionsfragen finden sich auf S. 86–87. Im Zusatzdownload sind die Impulse als Karten zum Ausdrucken aufbereitet.

Danke!

So ein Themenheft fällt nicht vom Himmel und allein ist das kaum zu schaffen. Deshalb kurz und knapp nur die wichtigsten und ohne bestimmte Reihenfolge:

Danke Andy, Mom und Dad, den beiden größten Kleinen, meinen Schüler*innen, Susanne, Natalie, Lauren, Sarah-Marie.

Ohne euch wäre das alles nicht so möglich gewesen.

The USA – An Overview

What is this chapter about?

In diesem Kapitel geht es um einen ersten Einblick in die Vereinigten Staaten: Was macht das Land aus? Welche Symbolik steckt hinter der weltberühmten Flagge, was hat ein Salat mit den USA zu tun und was meinen wir eigentlich, wenn wir vom „Mittleren Westen" sprechen?

Die Lernenden werden in diesem Kapitel dazu eingeladen, sich den USA zu nähern, ihr Vorwissen zu aktivieren und neue, lebensnahe Themen zu erkunden. Dazu findet sich für jedes Thema dieses Kapitels ein Informationsblatt, welches wissenswerte Fakten knapp zusammenfasst und Impulse zur Weiterarbeit geben kann. Auf den dazugehörigen Arbeitsblättern gibt es jeweils eine Aufgabenstellung, die eine tiefere und/oder affektive Auseinandersetzung mit dem Inhalt fördert.

Bitte achten Sie bei der Auseinandersetzung mit Kulturen darauf, auch innerhalb der Klasse keine Zuschreibungen vorzunehmen. Bei der Erstellung des „Celebration calender" (S. 13) sollten Schüler*innen nur von sich aus Feste teilen und es sollte vermieden werden, vom Aussehen oder von der Herkunft auf Religion oder vermeintliche Bräuche oder Feste zu schließen. Darüber hinaus sollte das Konzept „kulturelle Aneignung" („cultural appropriation") mit den Schüler*innen besprochen werden.

Die Inhalte bieten vielfältige Möglichkeiten der Weiterarbeit – gerade auch im bilingualen Unterricht. Angesichts der Fülle der Informationen, die schon bei einem knappen Überblick zusammenkommt, wurde in diesem Kapitel bewusst didaktisch reduziert:

☆ Von all den Symbolen, die für die USA typisch sind, wurde die Flagge gewählt.
☆ Die einzelnen Regionen der USA werden nicht im Detail, sondern exemplarisch an jeweils einem Staat erarbeitet.
☆ Das Konzept der USA als Melting Pot oder Salad Bowl wird kurz und schülergerecht erläutert.

Im Anschluss an die einzelnen Themen finden sich noch weitere Aufgabenideen, die eine vertiefte Auseinandersetzung ermöglichen („More creativity", S. 22–28). Sie können auch Aufgabenstellungen aus den einzelnen Themen durch diese ersetzen und im Mix-and-Match-Prinzip munter kombinieren.

The USA — An Overview

The United States of America

The USA is officially called "United States of America". It is a **union** of 50 different states. 49 of the states are located on the **mainland** and one state, Hawaii, is located in the Pacific Ocean. This makes Hawaii a popular travel **destination**. The capital of the USA is Washington D.C. where the president lives in the White House.
There are more than 330 million people in the USA. They come from different cultures and speak a lot of different languages. And although English and Spanish are spoken by a lot of people, there is no official language.

U.S. states

Geography

The USA is the second largest country on the North American continent. It shares land **borders** with Canada to the north and with Mexico to the south. The largest U.S. state – when looking at the land area – is Alaska. It is bigger than Germany, Austria, Switzerland, Italy and France combined! The USA is the only country to have all five major climate zones: tropical, dry, **temperate**, continental, and polar. And there are other geographical records: Lake Superior in the Midwest is the largest freshwater lake in the world, Mammoth Cave National Park has the world's longest **cave system** and if you want to travel to the hottest place on this planet, then you have to visit Death Valley. The highest temperature ever recorded there was 134 °F (53,7 °C).

National symbols

When you visit the USA, you will see it on display literally everywhere: the U.S. flag. With its 50 stars and 13 red and white stripes, people all over the world recognize it. The national bird is the **bald eagle**. You can find it on millions of dollar bills. People display these symbols to show how proud they are to be American and how much they love their country.

bald eagle

---

union: die Vereinigung, **mainland:** das Festland, **destination:** das Ziel, **border:** die Grenze, **temperate:** gemäßigt, **cave system:** das Höhlensystem, **bald eagle:** der Weißkopfseeadler

The USA — An Overview

The United States of America

⭐ ABC-list

1. Think:
What comes to your mind when you think about the United States of America? What do you already know? You have got 5 minutes to fill the ABC-list. Make sure the ideas you note down start with the letter given.

2. Together:
Compare your notes with a partner. Complete your lists with each other's help.

A ....

B ....

C ....

D ....

E ....

F ....

G ....

H ....

I ....

J ....

K ....

L ....

M ....

N ....

O ....

P ....

Q ....

R ....

S ....

T ....

U ....

V ....

W ....

X ....

Y ....

Z ....

The USA — An Overview

The Red, White and Blue

No flag is more famous across the world than the flag of the United States of America. It is full of symbols and carries a lot of meaning:

- **50 stars:** The stars represent the states that form the USA.
- **13 stripes:** The red stripes stand for the 13 original colonies that became **independent** from Great Britain in 1776.
- **Red:** The color red is a symbol for **courage** and strength.
- **White:** The color white symbolizes **purity** and **innocence**.
- **Blue:** The color blue stands for **vigilance**, **perseverance** and **justice**.

There are many nicknames for the American flag: "Stars and Stripes" **dates back to** 1809. It's quite **obvious** where that name comes from, right? The flag is also called "The Red, White and Blue". This term came up in different songs and is still used today. Some people also call the flag the "Star-Spangled Banner". This means that a flag is covered with bright stars. This name – which people widely use today – was first used in a poem by Francis Scott Key.

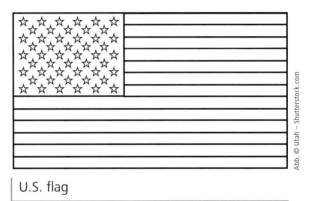

U.S. flag

Citizens of the USA tend to be very proud of their flag. You can find it on display at public institutions, schools and also at private homes. Since the flag is a very important symbol, there are several rules that people follow when using the flag. Here are some examples:

- The flag should only be out in the day. If it's out during the night, it should be **illuminated**.
- The flag should never touch anything beneath it: ground, floor or water.
- The flag should not be worn as a costume.
- When the flag is worn out, destroy it. It's best to burn it. Don't throw it in the trash.

> **independent:** unabhängig, **courage:** der Mut, **purity:** die Reinheit, **innocence:** die Unschuld, **vigilance:** die Wachsamkeit, **perseverance:** das Durchhaltevermögen, **justice:** die Gerechtigkeit, **to date back to:** zurückgehen auf etw., **obvious:** offensichtlich, **citizen:** der Bürger/die Bürgerin, **illuminated:** beleuchtet

The USA — An Overview

The Red, White and Blue

⭐ Creating your class flag

1. Think: Flags represent the culture of a nation, a club or a team. Look up some flags online and then come up with ideas for a flag that represents the culture of your class. These questions can help you:

☆ What is important to you?
☆ What makes you special as a group?
☆ What elements and symbols would you include? Why?
☆ Which name would best fit your flag?

2. Create: Draw the flag. Here are some symbols you could use:

Our class flag

name of flag: ....

3. Present: Present your ideas to your class.

The USA — An Overview

Mix it, baby!

The history of the USA is the story of millions of immigrants. Immigration often took place in waves – meaning that there were even more people coming to the States during specific times.

Have you ever heard people talking about the USA as a **melting pot**? This metaphor stands for a country and culture where people of different **origins** and from all over the world come together and "melt" together, becoming part of the American way of life and creating one united culture.

Today, we mostly refer to the USA as a "salad bowl". This metaphor **suggests** that people from different countries and with various cultures come together and combine their cultures. They mostly keep their own cultural identities.

Cultural mix today

Still today people try to find their own American Dream. They come to the USA to live a better life – whatever this might mean. You can find people with origins from all over the world in the USA. For example, there are large Chinese-American **communities** all across the U.S. A rich cultural tradition which **enslaved** Africans brought with them can still be found today and in some cities more than half of the population is **Hispanic**. On the one hand, people celebrate and practice their own culture: Indian-Americans celebrate Diwali, Mexican-Americans celebrate the Day of the Dead, and Chinese-Americans celebrate the Chinese New Year. On the other hand, people do **assimilate** when they come to the USA: They learn the English language and also take part in the celebration of national holidays like Independence Day or Thanksgiving.

---

melting pot: der Schmelztiegel, **origin:** der Ursprung, **to suggest:** nahelegen, **community:** die Gemeinschaft, **enslaved:** versklavt, **Hispanic:** im Zusammenhang mit Spanien bzw. Spanisch sprechenden Ländern Mittel- und Südamerikas stehend, **to assimilate:** sich angleichen

The USA — An Overview

Mix it, baby!

⭐ Celebration calendar

1. Think: Different cultures bring different celebrations. Which holidays and festivities do you and your family celebrate throughout the year? Take notes.

2. Together: Get together in groups of 3–4 students. Talk about the celebrations you collected. Design a celebration calendar for your class. Add the names of the holidays and celebrations and also use symbols and drawings to make your calendar stand out.

Tip: Use this worksheet to collect ideas and then create a big poster for your classroom!

January	February

March	April

May	June

July	August

September	October

November	December

The USA — An Overview

The Northeast — Massachusetts

Massachusetts is a state in the Northeast of the USA. It has a lot to offer: You can go skiing in the western Berkshire mountains or you can spend your vacation at the beautiful beaches of Cape Cod. If you're interested in culture, you should visit its capital Boston and the **surrounding** area to find museums or places for shopping. Want to learn something new? Drop by the famous Harvard University!

Massachusetts state flag

The name "Massachusetts" probably comes from the Massachusett **tribe** of Native Americans. It can be translated to "near the great hill" which refers to the Blue Hills southwest of Boston. Massachusetts also has a nickname: "the Bay State". This might come from all the **bays** that you can find in this state.

state bird: **black-capped chickadee**

Historical facts

The first people lived in what is now Massachusetts around 12,000 years ago. Later on, Native American tribes lived in the area. In 1620, a famous ship called the "Mayflower" brought people from England who created the first **permanent** European **settlement** there. Massachusetts has been in the center of many historic events: in the 17th century, **rumors** led to **witch hunts** during which more than 200 people **were accused of** practicing **witchcraft**. 20 of them were killed. Massachussetts also played a big role in the movement for **independence** from Great Britain.

state flower: Mayflower

Massachusetts is a state of "firsts". The first railway in the USA was built in Boston in 1795. The state is home to the first post office, the first public library and the first subway. In addition, it was the first U.S. state to legalize **same-sex marriage** in 2004.

---

surrounding: umliegend, **black-capped chickadee:** die Schwarzkopfmeise, **tribe:** der Volksstamm, **bay:** die Bucht, **permanent:** dauerhaft, **settlement:** die Siedlung, **rumor:** das Gerücht, **witch hunt:** die Hexenjagd, **to be accused of sth.:** beschuldigt werden, etwas getan zu haben, **witchcraft:** die Hexerei, **independence:** die Unabhängigkeit, **same-sex marriage:** die gleichgeschlechtliche Ehe

The USA — An Overview

The Northeast — Massachusetts

⭐ Creating a greeting card

Writing and sending loved ones a card has a long tradition in the USA — many Americans just LOVE sending cards on many **occasions**: birthdays, **graduation**, national holidays, Christmas and, of course, Valentine's Day. Funnily enough, the first mass-produced Valentine's cards and the first American Christmas cards were printed in Massachusetts.

1. Think: Brainstorm ideas in order to design your own greeting card:
☆ Which occasion is about to come up?
☆ Who would you like to send a card to?

2. Create: Design the outside of the card: Do you go for funny and clever or rather classic? Do you want to make it colorful or keep it simple? You can use the card in **upright format** or in **landscape format**. Just turn the worksheet.

3. Write: Note down your greetings first. What do you want to tell the **addressee** on this special occasion?

---

occasion: die Gelegenheit, **graduation:** der (Schul-)Abschluss, **upright format:** das Hochformat, **landscape format:** das Querformat, **addressee:** der Empfänger/die Empfängerin

The USA — An Overview

The Midwest – Indiana

highway sign in Indiana

Indiana is a typical flyover state. "Flyover country" and "flyover states" are American phrases that describe the parts of the United States between the East and the West Coast. They are often believed to be so boring that you best only see them from above when you're flying from one coast to the other. While this does not sound very nice, others call this **vast** region "heartland" – not only because it's in the middle of the USA but because it also has got lots of things to offer. The states of the heartland are also called "the Midwest".

 The name "Indiana" comes from the nations and **tribes** of Native Americans that lived there when the Europeans arrived.
The state probably gets its nickname "The Hoosier State" from an Old English word meaning "hill".

Indiana state flag

Historical facts

Native American nations and tribes lived on the land long before European **settlers** arrived. They left some pretty interesting objects that we can still see today. The French were the first Europeans to control the territory. It became a U.S. state in 1816.

 Just like other states, Indiana has state symbols that represent what is important to the state. The **cardinal** is its state bird and the **peony** the state flower.

state bird: cardinal

state flower: peony

vast: weit, **tribe:** der Volksstamm, **settler:** der Siedler/die Siedlerin, **cardinal:** der Rote Kardinal, **peony:** die Pfingstrose

The USA — An Overview

The Midwest – Indiana

⭐ Making the world a better place

Indianapolis is home to the world's biggest children's museum. One famous **exhibition** is about four children who changed the world: Anne Frank, Ruby Bridges, Ryan White and Malala Yousafzai. Ryan White was a young boy who was suffering from **hemophilia**. When a person has this disease, their blood doesn't **clot** the way it should, so that **wounds** and injuries will keep on bleeding and the patient has a lot of **bruises**. Hemophilia can be very dangerous and even lead to death.

Ryan was treated with blood transfusions and got infected with HIV. In the early 1980s, people were terrified of this new disease – they didn't really know a lot about it and misinformation was **widespread**. When Ryan wanted to go back to school, he wasn't allowed to. He fought to return to school and used the power of his voice to inform about AIDS.

Today there are also a lot of things going on in the world which are unfair and need people who use the power of their voices to change them.

1. Think: Which bad thing would you like to point out?
2. Create: Design a sticker with a short slogan. You can also include a symbol.
3. Write: Where would you like to stick it? Which places would reach a lot of people? Take notes first.
4. Present: Show your ideas to your class.

---

exhibition: die Ausstellung, **hemophilia:** die Hämophilie, die Bluterkrankheit, **to clot:** gerinnen, **wound:** die Wunde, **bruise:** der Bluterguss, **widespread:** weitverbreitet

The West – California

California is a state in the West of the U.S. on the Pacific Ocean. People have lived there for more than 20,000 years – the first people arrived on foot from Asia. They crossed the Bering Strait, a strip of land between today's Russia and the USA that is now covered with water.

state bird: California **valley** **quail**

In the 16th century Spanish **colonizers** came to this part of what now is the USA. After having been controlled by Mexico for some time, California became a U.S. **territory**. At the same time thousands of people came to California looking for gold. It has been a state since 1850.

Today, California is the state with the largest **population**. More than 39 million people live there. Its capital is Sacramento. The biggest city, however, is Los Angeles. Being home to Hollywood, California is the center of movie production in the USA.

 The name "California" comes from a bestselling 16th century novel. California probably gets its nickname "The Golden State" from the Gold Rush – when many people came there in search of gold – or from its state flower, the golden **poppy**, which can be found all over the state.

state flower: golden poppy

A state of extremes

Silicon Valley is a region in the south San Francisco Bay Area. It is home to hundreds of companies, most of them tech companies like Google, Meta and Apple. Silicon Valley is extremely rich – even one of the **wealthiest** regions in the world!

California has the highest point (Mount Whitney) and the lowest point (Badwater Basin in the Death Valley National Park) on the **contiguous** U.S. mainland. Moreover, Death Valley, located in the Mojave Desert, is the hottest place on earth.

> **colonizer:** der Besiedler/die Besiedlerin, **territory:** (Hoheits-)Gebiet, **population:** die Bevölkerung, **valley:** das Tal, **quail:** die Wachtel, **poppy:** der Mohn, **wealthy:** wohlhabend, **contiguous:** zusammenhängend

The USA – An Overview

The West – California

⭐ Inventing the future

1. Think: Imagine you were working at a fancy tech company in Silicon Valley. You come up with a smartphone which has one extremely useful new feature. Which feature is it? Why do people need it? And how could you sell it to the people?

2. Create: Design an ad for this **innovative** product. The words below may help you.

---

innovative: neuartig, **device:** das Gerät, der Apparat, **breakthrough:** der Durchbruch, **to develop:** entwickeln, **voice recording:** die Sprachaufnahme, **notification:** die Benachrichtigung, **invention:** die Erfindung, **up-to-date:** modern, **user-friendly:** benutzerfreundlich, **state of the art:** die aktuelle Technik, **useful:** nützlich

The USA — An Overview

The South — Louisiana

Lousiana is a state in the South of the USA. Like the other Southern states, it is very diverse and has its own **distinctive** culture. The climate is warm and so **crops** like **sugar cane**, rice, and **cotton** have been grown here for centuries. In the past – without big machines for farming the land – a lot of workers were needed to farm the land. **Enslaved** Africans were brought to the region as cheap **laborers** – a dark chapter in the history of the USA and especially the South.

Louisiana state flag

In 1682, France **laid claim to** this part of the country and it was named after King Louis XIV. Lousiana gets its nickname "The Pelican State" from its state bird, which you can also see on the state flag.

A mix of cultures

state flower: magnolia

The **ancestors** of the Cajun people came from France and first settled in Canada. In 1755, they lost their home to the British in a war and went to live in Louisiana. But you can still find their culture, for example in Cajun food which is a mixture of different traditions – and pretty **spicy**. Jambalaya and Gumbo are two famous **dishes**. Creole culture is another important part of Louisiana. In the past, people with ancestors from Spain and France were called Creoles. The most famous Creole tradition is the celebration of Mardi Gras in New Orleans. More than 1.5 million people come to visit the city then! There were also Native American and African influences. Most of the enslaved people were brought to Louisiana from West Africa. Their own **beliefs** mixed with the beliefs of Catholicism and brought up a new form of religious practice: the Louisiana voodoo. It is still **practiced** today.

---

distinctive: charakteristisch, **crop:** die Nutzpflanze, **sugar cane:** das Zuckerrohr, **cotton:** die Baumwolle, **enslaved:** verslavt, **laborer:** der Arbeiter/die Arbeiterin, **to lay claim to sth.:** Anspruch auf etw. erheben, **ancestor:** der Vorfahre/die Vorfahrin, **spicy:** würzig, **dish:** das Gericht, **belief:** der Glaube, **to practice:** ausüben

The USA — An Overview

The South — Louisiana

⭐ Creating a Mardi Gras mask

Masks are one of the most loved Mardi Gras traditions. For centuries people of different societies have worn masks for celebrations and rituals and Mardi Gras wouldn't be the same without them.

In the beginning of Mardi Gras celebrations, people wore masks to **escape** the rules of **society**: people from lower classes could get together with ones from upper classes and everyone could be who they wanted to be. To this day Mardi Gras is still an exciting celebration.

1. Create: Design your own mask. Add feathers, **beads**, **gems** … Choose which colors you want to use. Which meaning do they carry for you?

2. Present: Present your mask to the class.

to escape: entkommen, entfliehen, **society:** die Gesellschaft, **bead:** die Perle, **gem:** der Schmuckstein

The USA — An Overview

More creativity

⭐ Profiles and Travel Guide

1. Research: Gather information about another U.S. state, for example Hawaii, New Mexico, Alaska, Colorado, Mississippi, Pennsylvania, New Jersey, or Rhode Island. Of course, you can also choose any other state. The "How to: Research" box below can help you.

2. Create: Design either a profile or a collage about it. The respective "How to" boxes can help you.

3. Together: Create a travel guide of the U.S. combining all your class's works.

How to: Research

If you want to use the internet for research, you can try the following keywords to use in the search engine:
(state name) history, (state name) basic facts, (state name) symbols, (state name) fun facts, (state name) sights, (state name) wildlife, …

How to: Collage

A collage is a piece of art about your state. People want to see more than they want to read. Search for pictures and photos. Which pictures and photos complement the information that you want to give? Cut them out.
Arrange the cutouts and glue them on a sheet of paper. Add information that you want to give – but keep it short!
Use symbols and drawings to make your collage more interesting.

How to: Profile

What if your state was a gangster and you had to create a profile with the most important information so that the police could find it? Which information would you include? And which one or two photos would be absolutely necessary?
Research the information. Add one or two photos. Make your profile graphic and relatively "clean". You can organize the information in boxes.

How to: Travel Guide

You are to design a travel guide for a trip from the West Coast to the East Coast.
In which order would you suggest visiting the different states? Put the profiles of your states in the order you're suggesting. Also think of a name for your travel guide.
Make a design contest for the best cover design. Collect the different cover suggestions and vote for the best one.
You might also want to include a map of the USA and highlight the places to visit.

The USA — An Overview

More creativity

⭐ Creating a license plate

When you're traveling on an American highway, you should take a good look at the license plates. They can be really creative, interesting and funny even. How about creating your own license plate?

1. Research: Which state do you want your license plate to be from? Choose one from the photo or think of a different one. Look for more information on the state online. What's an interesting fact about it?

2. Think: Brainstorm and take short notes first:
- ☆ Which name, letters, or number combinations would you like to be on the license plate?
- ☆ Which motto could go with the interesting fact? Make up a state motto to go on your license plate.
- ☆ Think of pictures, icons or symbols that would go well with your license plate.

3. Create: Design your license plate below.

The USA — An Overview

More creativity

⭐ Creating a brochure

1. Research: Find out more about another state of the USA. Create a travel brochure for it. Your research could include:

- ☆ location and climate
- ☆ sights and monuments
- ☆ fun activities on land and water
- ☆ places to stay (camping sites, hotels, …)
- ☆ celebrations throughout the year

2. Create: Design an interesting cover to get people's attention. You can use different ways of folding for your brochure. Remember: Also include pictures and photos.

How to: Brochure – research

If you want to use the internet for research, you can try the following keywords to use in the search engine:
(state name) fun activities, (state name) activities for kids, (state name) museums, (state name) landmarks, (state name) sights, (state name) celebrations, (state name) climate …

How to: Brochure – tri fold

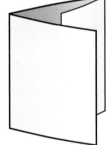

Put the paper in front of you horizontally. Use a ruler to divide the length of the paper into thirds and mark the lines. Fold both flaps along the lines. The flaps both cover the center.
This brochure is great if you want to have a "secret" or special message in the center. The message will only be seen when the brochure is completely open.

How to: Brochure – center fold

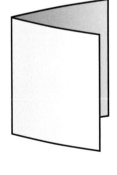

This is the most basic fold. Lay the paper in front of you horizontally. Fold it in half. You have now got a brochure which looks like a book cover with no pages inside.
This brochure is great if you want to use a lot of pictures and not as much text.

How to: Brochure – Z fold

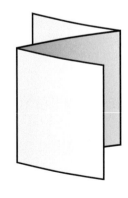

Put your paper in front of you horizontally. Use a ruler to divide the length of the paper into thirds and mark the lines. Now take the left panel and fold it along the line to the right. Then take the right panel and fold it to the back of the brochure.
You now will have an accordion-like structure. This brochure is great if you want to put a lot of information into it. It also gives you a lot of different sections to structure the information.

The USA — An Overview

More creativity

★ Scavenger Hunt (1/2)

1. Riddle: Find out some interesting facts about the different states of the USA. Read through the questions below. Research the answers on the internet if you don't know them already. Find the state on the map (on page 2). Write down the letters to get the solution sentence.

Questions

1. Which state is more than double the size of Texas?
2. In which U.S. state can you find the "Maid of the **Mist**", a real wonder of the world?
3. In which state can you find the "sweetest place on Earth"?
4. Can you find out which state has the most **lighthouses**?
5. The first airplane flight ever took place in …
6. The only place where alligators and crocodiles exist in the same spot is in …
7. Higher and higher: The world's first **skyscraper** was built in …
8. In which state can you walk on a glass bridge in the shape of a **horseshoe** more than 1,200 meters above the ground?
9. The world's oldest trees can be found in …
10. Which state is home to a **colossal** sculpture showing the faces of four U.S. presidents?
11. This state is home to the biggest ranch of the USA. It's bigger than the state of Rhode Island!
12. Which state has a picture of the largest **mammal** in North America on its flag?

2. Research: The solution will be a typical American **saying**. Find out what it means.

The saying means ....

....

---

scavenger hunt: die Schnitzeljagd, **mist:** der Nebel, **lighthouse:** der Leuchtturm, **skyscraper:** der Wolkenkratzer, **horseshoe:** das Hufeisen, **colossal:** riesig, **mammal:** das Säugetier, **saying:** das Sprichwort

The USA — An Overview

Scavenger Hunt (2/2)

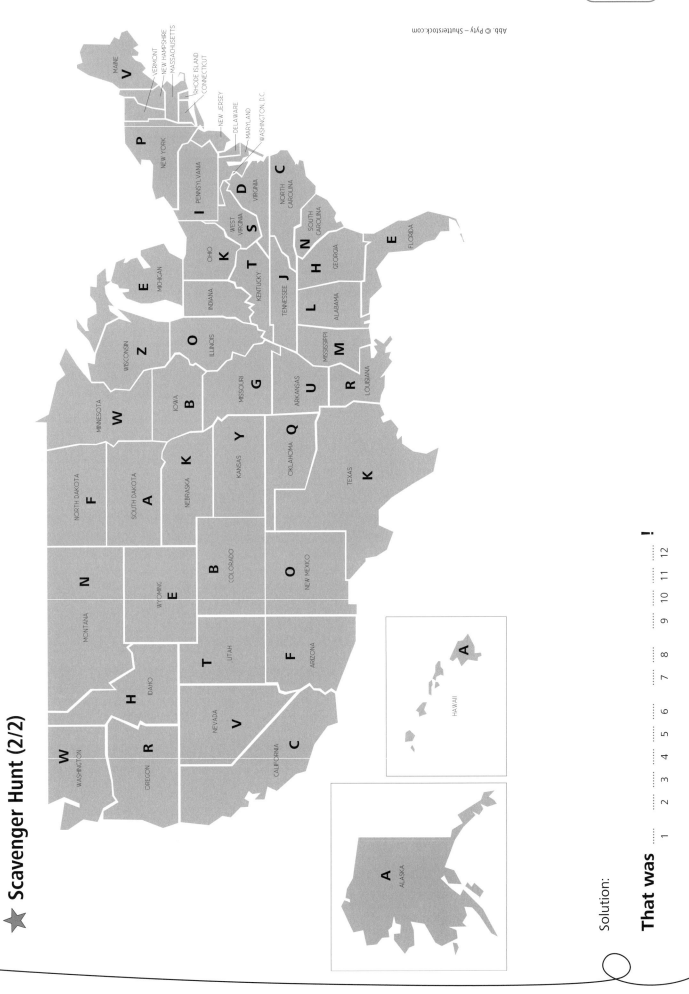

Solution:

That was __ __ __ __ __ __ __ __ __ __ __ __ !
         1 2 3 4 5 6 7 8 9 10 11 12

The USA — An Overview

More creativity

⭐ Creating a podcast (1/2)

1. Think: What is similar and what is different when you compare the USA and Germany? Take notes first.

2. Together: Create a podcast episode about the differences that young Americans could be most interested in. Brainstorm your ideas first. Write your ideas into the thought bubbles below.
☆ Which topics will they be most interested in?
☆ What is important information that you would like to give them?

The USA — An Overview

⭐ Creating a podcast (2/2)

3. Together: Write out your episode. You can take notes only or write complete sentences – whatever works best for you. Also think of a name for your podcast and the episode.

4. Present: Either record your episode or be ready to present it in front of the class.

name of podcast: ....

name of episode: ....

Cities and Sights

What is this chapter about?

Städte und Sehenswürdigkeiten der USA – wo fängt man an, wo hört man auf? Mit unzähligen Orten voller Geschichte und Geschichten und einer überwältigenden Anzahl spektakulärer Naturlandschaften ist es gar nicht so leicht, eine Auswahl zu treffen, die einerseits der Vielfalt gerecht wird und gleichzeitig Lernende in ihrer Lebenswelt abholt und außerdem die Möglichkeit bietet, an Vorwissen anzuknüpfen.

Die hier vorgestellten Städte haben selbst schon fast Kultstatus und sind unseren Schüler*innen sicher nicht gänzlich unbekannt. Kurze Infos zu jeder Stadt finden sich jeweils auf den Informationsblättern. Diese laden dazu ein, sich durch einfaches Lesen, das Lesen im Wechsel oder auch das Übersetzen einzelner Abschnitte der Geschichte und Kultur der jeweiligen Stadt anzunähern. Auch die Vielzahl an Nationalparks und die beeindruckenden Niagara-Fälle bekommen in diesem Kapitel ihren Raum.

Im Anschluss an die Erarbeitung der Inhalte des Infoblatts findet sich jeweils eine kreative Aufgabe, die allein, in Partner- oder auch in Gruppenarbeit bearbeitet werden kann. Dabei entwickeln die Lernenden eigene Ideen und setzen sich so intensiv und in der Zielsprache mit neuen Blickwinkeln auseinander.

Am Ende des Kapitels finden Sie eine Auswahl an kreativen Aufgabenformen, die sich nicht zwangsläufig an eine bestimmte Thematik des Kapitels anschließen müssen. Sie ermöglichen stattdessen die intensive Arbeit an einem Produkt – mit besonderem Fokus auf Kreativität und Kollaboration – und sind somit als Projektarbeit bestens geeignet. Die Aufgabenstellungen benötigen in ihrer Umsetzung durchaus etwas Zeit und bieten damit einen guten Rahmen, um Lern- und Arbeitsprozesse zu beobachten und das fertige Produkt anhand festgelegter Kriterien zu beurteilen. Für die kreativen Aufgabenformen findet sich eine „assessment scale" (S. 50), welche für die Lernenden Transparenz in eine mögliche Beurteilung bringt und sich an dem 4K-Modell des Lernens orientiert.

Abb. © Yanina Nosova – Shutterstock.com

Cities and Sights

New York City

New York City is often called "the culture capital of the world". It's home to many different cultures – making it one of the most international cities with more than 800 different languages spoken. Here, you can find and **explore** art, cultures and food from all around the world. This **unique** mixture makes NYC a popular travel destination for millions of visitors each year.

 New York City has got a lot of different nicknames: "the Big Apple", "the City That Never Sleeps", "Gotham" or simply "the City". There are five **boroughs**: the Bronx, Brooklyn, Queens, Manhattan and Staten Island. The most well-known sight of the United States is right here in NYC: the Statue of Liberty.

Museums, galleries and theaters

New York City is very rich when it comes to museums and art galleries. In the more than 100 museums you can **admire** some of the most famous works of art, look at dinosaur skeletons or learn about history and **aviation**. Over 1,000 art galleries show works from all across the world. If you enjoy going to theaters, you'll also find lots of places to visit in New York City. Including the famous theaters on Broadway, there are hundreds of theaters to go to and watch all kinds of plays including the well-liked theaters on Broadway.

Shopping, dining and having fun

If you've got some money to spend on luxury shopping, you have to visit Fifth Avenue in Manhattan. More than 10 kilometers long, it's one of the world's most expensive streets when it comes to the **rent** per year. You can mainly find **flagship stores** of famous **brands** there. With more than 20,000 restaurants all over New York City there are new delicious experiences waiting for you on every corner. And if you feel like dancing and celebrating, then just keep your eyes open for different festivals taking place all year round.

---

to explore sth.: etw. entdecken, **unique:** einzigartig, **borough:** der Stadtteil, **to admire:** bewundern, **aviation:** die Luftfahrt, **rent:** die Miete, **flagship store:** die Vorzeigefiliale eines Handelsunternehmens, **brand:** die Marke

Cities and Sights

New York City

⭐ Water tower art

Some well-known NYC icons are the water towers. They can be found on top of high buildings, making sure that also the upper floors get fresh water. It takes about 24 hours to build one and they can last up to 35 years. Only three **family-run businesses** build and **maintain** the more than 15,000 water towers in all of NYC.

The water towers are also of cultural interest. During the spring of 2013, 300 rooftop water tanks were transformed into art by **established** artists, as well as newcomers and even students of New York City public schools. The idea behind "The Water Tank Project" was **to raise awareness** that water is a very **precious** resource.

water tower in Brooklyn

1. Think: You get to design a water tank in NYC. Which fact or problem would you like to raise awareness for? Take notes.

2. Create: What would your water tank look like? Draw your design below.

3. Present: Talk about your ideas in class.

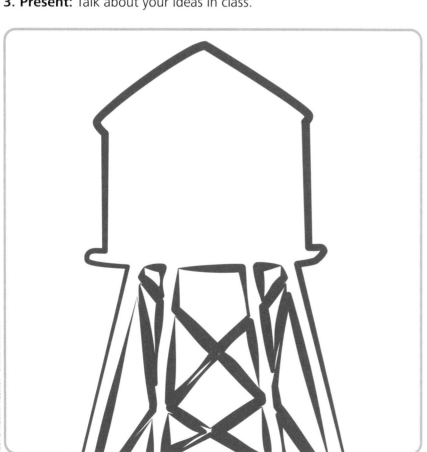

family-run business: das Familienunternehmen,
to maintain: instandhalten,
established: etabliert,
to raise awareness: Bewusstsein wecken,
precious: wertvoll

Cities and Sights

Chicago

Chicago is the third largest city in the USA. It's located on Lake Michigan, which gives it 28 miles of **lakefront**.

Brief history

Before European settlers came along, the area was home to the Algonquian **tribes**. The name "Chigagou" came from their language and means "onion field". A **trapper** named Jean Baptiste Point du Sable built a **settlement** and **trading post** there in the 1770s. This little settlement then would grow into a town and later on a city.

Chicago **hosted** The Chicago World's Fair in 1893. It was a large **exhibition** where different nations could show their achievements and new inventions. The politicians of Chicago tried everything to bring the fair into their city – so they talked about Chicago being a special and wonderful place. A reporter from New York called them "full of hot air" because of their **bragging**. Maybe this is the reason why Chicago is called "The Windy City" – or it might just be the cool winds coming from Lake Michigan. Chicago also has a great history of music, especially jazz, and was home to gangster bosses throughout the Prohibition, a time when it was illegal to sell alcohol.

Things to see and do

There are a lot of attractions and sights to visit when you're in Chicago: Let's go to the famous Willis Tower and look down on the city from a glass balcony on the 103rd floor. It used to be the world's highest building and its **elevators** are still among the fastest in the world.

Chicago-Style Deep Dish Pizza

Have a tour on stand-up **scooters** that take you to interesting sights like the Millennium Park, **admire** Chicago's architecture while taking a river cruise tour, visit one of the many museums where you can look at art or learn about natural history, or go to Navy Pier for some cool places to eat or adventurous **rides**.

---

lakefront: das Seeufer, **tribe:** der Volksstamm, **trapper:** der Pelztier-Jäger, die Pelztier-Jägerin, **settlement:** die Siedlung, **trading post:** der Handelsposten, **to host:** ausrichten, **exhibition:** die Ausstellung, **to brag:** angeben, **elevator:** der Aufzug, **scooter:** der Roller, **to admire:** bewundern, **ride:** das Fahrgeschäft

Cities and Sights

Chicago

⭐ **Become a gangster tour guide! (1/2)**

Chicago was home to many gangsters including the famous "Scarface" Al Capone. He made money from illegal actions like **smuggling** and selling alcohol during the **Prohibition**. Imagine you were to give a gangster tour visiting some of Capone's favorite Chicago places.

Al Capone

1. Research: Do some research on one of Chicago's Capone places. Choose one from the list below. Find out how it is linked to Capone and Chicago's gangster history.

> The Lexington Hotel Chicago • The Blackstone Hotel Chicago •
> The Green Mill Chicago • The Exchequer Restaurant Chicago

2. Think: You will slip into the role of a gangster tour guide. What would you like to tell the tourists about your place? Answer the following questions before making up a story to tell them.
- ☆ What kind of place is it?
- ☆ Where is it? Is it more of a secret place or is it full of people?
- ☆ When would Capone go there?
- ☆ Whom would he meet there? His family and friends? Business partners or people to do his dirty work?
- ☆ What would he feel like at this place?
- ☆ How would the other people feel when they saw him?
- ☆ How would Capone behave at this place? Would he be relaxed and funny? Or rather **grim** and **strict**?

3. Write: Put your notes into a **captivating** story. Use the "Storyteller tactics" and "Sentence beginnings" (page 2) for help.

4. Present: Tell your story to your class or record it.

---

smuggling: der Schmuggel, **Prohibition:** eine Zeit, während der die Herstellung und der Verkauf von Alkohol in den USA illegal waren, **grim:** grimmig, **strict:** streng, unnachgiebig, **captivating:** fesselnd

Cities and Sights

Become a gangster tour guide! (2/2)

Storyteller tactics

1. Choose your main character. Is it Capone himself? Or a maybe little girl that watches him? How old is the main character? What makes them special? What do they look like? Are they afraid of something? What do they want? What are their names? Think of an interesting point of view.

2. Think of an antagonist. A good story always needs a bad person. Is Capone the antagonist? Or the police officer who wants to catch him? Or maybe even a little boy who wants to `rat` Capone `out` to the police? How old are they? What do they want? What do they look like? What are they called?

3. Sketch the place where your story takes place in every detail. Think of adjectives to describe it: Is it loud? Crowded? Dim? Maybe it's got a friendly atmosphere? Which time of day is it? What do the other people do there?

4. Think of an unexpected event that happens. Is it positive or negative? Does it have something to do with the antagonist? How does it change the story?

5. Structure your story. You can use the sentence beginnings below.

6. Boost your story: Does your hero have a friend or partner to count on? Are they in love? Why does the antagonist behave like that? Include some difficulties for your main character and even a moment of despair. What do they learn in the end?

Sentence beginnings

It was a normal day/evening/night …

And then one day …

He/she/they had to do something!

But all of a sudden …

In the end, …

> **to rat out:** verraten, verpfeifen

Cities and Sights

Los Angeles

Los Angeles is a city on the western coast of the USA. Los Angeles **county** features some of the most beautiful coastlines and best surfing spots, like Santa Monica, Venice Beach and Malibu. L.A. is said to have "perfect weather" with lots of sunshine, almost no rain and nice ocean **breezes** during the hot summer – a fact which attracts both tourists and new **residents**.

Hollywood

Hollywood sign

What would L.A. be without Hollywood? Hollywood is a **district** in the city of Los Angeles and home to the American film industry. The famous Hollywood sign was put up as an **advertisement** for a **housing development** and said "Hollywoodland" at first. Today it's so iconic that a visit to L.A. is not complete without taking a selfie with it.

Things to see and do

Are you a movie fan? Then you should definitely go to the Universal Studios – make sure to carefully plan your visit because there are just too many things to see! Explore the world of Harry Potter, experience Halloween horror, meet the dinosaurs of the Jurassic World or spend some time with Super Mario. Enjoy adventurous **rides** or relax in one of the many restaurants.

If you want to feel even closer to the stars, then you could book a tour that brings you outside celebrities' homes. Maybe you'll even see a movie star take out the **garbage**? Are you an **aspiring** actor or actress yourself? Then you probably dream about having your own star on the "Hollywood Walk of Fame". Your name would then be up for everyone to see – next to more than 2,700 other famous people's names you know from the radio, television or music.

> **county:** der Landkreis, **breeze:** die Brise, **resident:** der Bewohner/die Bewohnerin, **district:** der Bezirk, **advertisement:** die Werbung, **housing development:** der Siedlungsbau, **ride:** das Fahrgeschäft, **garbage:** der Müll, **aspiring:** aufstrebend

Cities and Sights

Los Angeles

⭐ Who am I?

In 2023, The Walt Disney Company celebrated its 100th birthday. Disney – as one of the most important players in the Hollywood Dream Factory – has played a major role in the childhood of generations. Which are your favorite Disney characters?

1. Think: Play a game! Think of a name of a Disney movie character. Write the character's name on a scrap of paper and fold it in half. Use the internet for research if you're not sure about each and every detail of the character.

2. Together: Get together in groups of four to five people or have a person sit on the "hot-seat" in front of the class. The person whose turn it is picks a scrap of paper without looking at the name written on it and shows it to the others without looking at it themselves.

The person now has to ask questions in order to find out who they are. You can start off with questions like "Am I a **villain**?", "How old am I?", "Am I human or an animal?". The words from the box can help you.

Keep track of the amount of questions that the player has to ask until they found out who they are. Then take turns and see if someone else can find their character faster.

---

villain: der Bösewicht, **human:** der Mensch, menschlich, **male:** männlich, der Mann, **female:** weiblich, die Frau, **superpower:** die Superkraft, **extraterrestrial:** außerirdisch, **strong:** stark, **clever:** schlau, **loving:** liebevoll

Cities and Sights

Las Vegas

Las Vegas is a city in the state of Nevada. It's right in the Mojave Desert and Nevada's **economic** center. There are numerous casinos, hotels and entertainment **venues** which make it a popular tourist attraction: More than 40 million people visited Las Vegas in 2023! But it's not only a place of positive superlatives. Like in every large city, there are also some **downsides** to find.

Along Las Vegas's **downtown's** main street – the so-called "Strip" – you can find all sorts of entertainment: casinos, shows, the largest glass pyramid in the world (as part of the Luxor hotel) and some of the biggest and most expensive hotels. There are hotels with adventurous rides on their **rooftops** and a lot of them follow a special theme: "The Venetian", for example, has copies of attractions from the Italian city of Venice – you can even ride a **gondola** on a canal!

But that's not all: Each luxury hotel is also home to shopping boutiques, restaurants and casinos – you won't even have to set foot outside in order to get the full Las Vegas experience! Las Vegas is also the world's wedding capital with more than 150 weddings per day.

the iconic Las Vegas sign

The downsides

Las Vegas is also an ordinary Western city that attracts thousands of new **residents** each year. This growth and the fact that the city gets its **wealth** by being a "**Sin City**" causes some problems: Criminal rates are amongst the highest in the country, **suicide** rates are also high, as is alcohol and illegal drug use. Furthermore, the city also has to deal with heavy traffic causing traffic jams and air pollution. Also, the fact that Las Vegas is in the middle of the Mojave desert makes water a **rare good**.

> **economic:** wirtschaftlich, **venue:** der Veranstaltungsort, **downside:** die Kehrseite, **downtown:** das Stadtzentrum, **rooftop:** das Dach, **gondola:** die Gondel, **resident:** der Bewohner/die Bewohnerin, **wealth:** der Reichtum, **Sin City:** Stadt der Sünde, **suicide:** der Suizid, **rare good:** das knappe Gut

Cities and Sights

Las Vegas

★ Between dollars and drought

Las Vegas gets most of its fresh water from Lake Mead – an **artificial** lake that is formed by the Hoover Dam and the Colorado River. Due to climate change and the growing population, there won't be enough water in the future to **supply** the city with what it needs. So, Las Vegas, therefore, has come up with plans to **conserve** water.

You are to help with designing a **billboard** for a campaign. The goal is to make people aware of **water waste** and that they can do a lot to help conserve water.

1. Think: First, brainstorm ways to save water. Keep in mind where people use water on a daily basis: personal hygiene, garden, washing the car, private pools, spare time activities (e.g. golfing) etc. Also think about what the geographical features of Las Vegas are like.

2. Create: Design your billboard.

3. Present: Talk about your ideas in class.

> **artificial:** künstlich, **to supply sb. with sth.:** jmd. mit etw. versorgen, **to conserve:** etw. einsparen, **billboard:** die Plakatwand, **water waste:** die Wasserverschwendung

Cities and Sights

National parks

There aren't many things that are more **distinctive** for the USA than their national parks. All in all, there are 63 parks which together cover an area of roughly 210,000 square kilometers – that is almost as big as all of the UK!

And there is more: The National Park Service does not only take care of the 63 parks with the goal to **preserve** nature and **wildlife**. They also look after sites documenting historic events and telling American stories: from the first people living on the continent 12,000 years ago up to today's diverse culture. Additionally, they want to bring **recreation** and education to a wide range of people. And they are highly successful: In 2022, more than 89 million visits to the 63 national parks were counted.

Famous parks

Among the most popular national parks are
- ☆ the Grand Canyon which is **roughly** 450 kilometers long,
- ☆ Yellowstone National Park which is the oldest National Park in the world,
- ☆ Redwood National Park where you can see giant redwood trees – so big that a car can drive right through them,
- ☆ Great Smoky Mountains National Park which is America's most visited national park with more than 12 million visitors per year.

The least visited national park

If you want to go to Gates of the Arctic National Park and Preserve you have to be up for a true wilderness experience. Up north in Alaska, you'll find no roads, no paths, no **cell service** and no **established** campsites. It is so **remote** that you can't go there by car: You must either **hike** or fly into the park. Only a little over 7,000 people seek this adventure per year – and they can spend days or weeks in the park before seeing another person!

---

distinctive: charakteristisch, **to preserve sth.:** etw. erhalten, **wildlife:** die Tierwelt, **recreation:** die Erholung, **roughly:** ungefähr, **cell service:** der Handyempfang, **established:** bestehend, eingerichtet, **remote:** abgelegen, **to hike:** wandern

Cities and Sights

National parks

⭐ Creating a Junior Ranger Badge

Most of the national parks offer a program where children can complete different activities during their stay at the park. They'll then receive a badge and a Junior Ranger Certificate.

Now, you get to design a Junior Ranger Badge for Yellowstone National Park!

1. Research: Before you start, find out: What is special about Yellowstone? What are some of its **distinctive** features? How could you include them on the badge so that everyone will recognize them right away? Would you like it to be colorful or black and white? Collect your ideas in a mindmap.

2. Create: Design your badge.

3. Present: Talk about your ideas in class.

> **ranger:** der Parkaufseher/die Parkaufseherin, **badge:** das Abzeichen, **distinctive:** charakteristisch

Cities and Sights

Niagara Falls

Niagara Falls **is comprised of** three waterfalls: the **Horseshoe** Falls, the American Falls and the **Bridal Veil** Falls. The biggest of the three – Horseshoe Falls – is on both the American and the Canadian side of the border. The other two are situated in the state of New York.

- During the summer and fall, more than 700,000 gallons of water **rush** down Niagara Falls per second – that's more than 2 million liters!
- The Falls do not freeze in the winter – but in 1848, their flow was just a small **trickle** for a few hours because ice had blocked the Niagara River further **upstream**.
- Niagara Falls is more than 12,000 years old.
- Niagara Falls is up to 187 feet high in some areas – this is around 57 meters!
- Most fish survive traveling down the waterfalls because of their ability to "go with the flow" – isn't that amazing?

Experiencing the Falls

There are different interesting tours you can take to really get a feel of the Falls – an experience you will probably never forget! A boat tour on the "Maid of the **Mist**" brings you close to the foot of the Falls. These tours have been offered since the 1840s. You are given a poncho to keep you dry, but you should also plan to wear waterproof shoes and clothes because the poncho might just not be enough.

If you want to take a different perspective on the Falls, then you can take a "Journey Behind the Falls". You'll first be taken to an observation deck from which you can see the Horseshoe Falls and the Niagara River. After that you'll walk down tunnels and **caves** until finding yourself right behind the **roaring** water.

> **to be comprised of:** aus etw. gebildet werden, **horseshoe:** das Hufeisen, **bridal veil:** der Brautschleier, **to rush:** rauschen, **trickle:** das Rinnsal, **upstream:** flussaufwärts, **mist:** der Nebel, **cave:** die Höhle, **roaring:** rauschend, tosend

Cities and Sights

Niagara Falls
⭐ Taking the plunge

 Daredevils at Niagara Falls are people who "take the plunge" – meaning they go down the Horseshoe Falls and hope that they will survive. Only 16 people have survived the plunge – no wonder that going down the Falls is strictly forbidden. The first person to go down Niagara Falls was a woman. Her name was Annie Edson Taylor. In 1901, she used a **barrel** which she called "Queen of the Mist" … and survived!

1. Research: Look for information on Annie Edson Taylor and her plunge online and take notes:
- ☆ Who was she? How old was she?
- ☆ Why did she take the plunge?
- ☆ What was special about her plunge?
- ☆ What did she say about it afterwards?

2. Create: Make up a social media post about her. Print out or draw a picture of her that represents her well. Then write a **caption** describing her and her adventures.

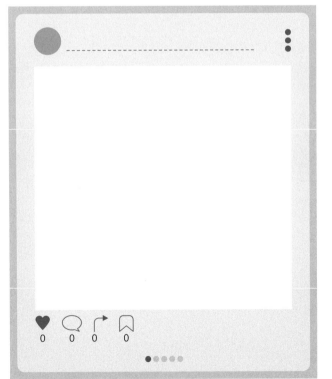

to take the plunge: den Sprung wagen, **daredevil:** der/die Draufgänger/in, **barrel:** das Fass, **caption:** die Bildunterschrift

Cities and Sights

More creativity

⭐ Collaborative writing (1/3)

1. Together: Work together in groups of 4–5 people. Imagine you were on vacation in the USA. You write about it in a blog entry for your school website.
Follow the steps below.

Attention: This task is an assignment for your group as a whole. Carefully outline and create your story together.

I. Roll the dice to find your story's beginning.

	When?	Who?	What?	Where?
⚀	It was early in the morning when …	… our families …	… took a walk …	… at Fisherman's Wharf.
⚁	On a rainy and rather cool afternoon …	… our tour guide …	… saw an interesting animal …	… next to General Sherman.
⚂	Late in the evening …	… a lady with curly hair …	… met a real star …	… in the Mall of America.
⚃	It was the first day of our vacation when …	… a new friend we had just made …	… left the hotel to go shopping …	… at the UFO Watchtower.
⚄	It was a really hot and sunny day when …	… we …	… ran away …	… near the Gateway Arch.
⚅	It was a special holiday over here when …	… the strange man in front of us …	… started singing …	… at the Martin Luther King, Jr. Memorial.

▷ Our story's first sentence is:

....

Cities and Sights

⭐ Collaborative writing (2/3)

II. Do some research.

▷ Where in the USA is the sight you're writing about?

....

▷ What important and interesting information can you find out about it?

....

....

▷ What can you do there?

....

....

III. Together, decide what will happen next. Make sure to develop a story with as many paragraphs as you have members in your group. Each team member will write their own paragraph. Outline your story in the boxes below: For example: If there are four people in your group, your blog post needs to have four paragraphs. Each paragraph should highlight a different scene of your story.

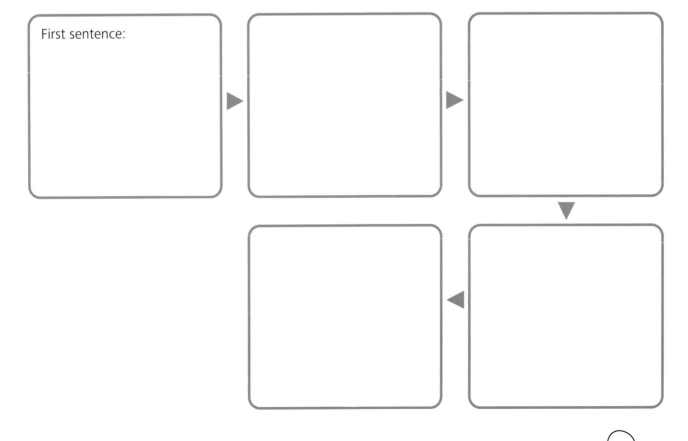

First sentence:

Cities and Sights

⭐ Collaborative writing (3/3)

IV. Write your own paragraph. Write about 10–15 sentences. Add adjectives to make your blog entry nice to read.

V. Give your first version to a partner. Have your partner make comments in the forms of symbols:

♥ = I like this!

❓ = I don't understand this part yet.

❗ = I think you made a mistake here.

VI. Rewrite your paragraph with the help of your partner's comments.

VII. Get together in your group and have a look at each other's paragraphs. Link the different paragraphs so that they make sense together.

VIII. Decide on a heading. Keep it short. Don't give away too much information.

IX. Call-to-action: Provoke a reaction! Ask your readers a question like: "What would you've done?" or "Have you ever been in a situation where … ?"

Checklist for the final result:

◯ Each member wrote a paragraph of 10–15 sentences.

◯ The paragraphs are linked.

◯ You included adjectives that make reading your story interesting.

◯ You found a captivating heading.

◯ You included a call-to-action.

Cities and Sights

More creativity

⭐ Creating a game (1/2)

1. Together: Get together in groups. You will design a board game that will take its players to some of the most interesting sights in the USA. First, talk about games that you like to play. Decide on which kind of game you want to create: Do you want to design a card game or a board game?

2. Research: Do some research on 4–6 of the sights in the box below that sound most interesting to you.
For example: Where are they? What is special about them? How many people visit them each year?

Sights you could include:

1 The Space Needle	12 Pearl Harbor	21 Fredrick Douglass National Historic Site
2 The Golden Gate Bridge	13 The Lincoln Memorial	22 National Civil Rights Museum
3 Corn Palace	14 Arlington National Cemetery	23 Taos Pueblos
4 Brooklyn Bridge	15 Mount Rushmore	24 The Enchanted Highway
5 U.S. Capitol Building	16 Independence National Historic Park	25 The Freedom Trail
6 Women's Rights National Historic Park	17 Statue of Liberty	26 Montezuma Castle
7 The Empire State Building	18 Harriet Tubman National Historic Park	27 Little Bighorn Battlefield
8 The White House	19 Alcatraz	28 Washington Monument
9 Gettysburg	20 Colonial Williamsburg	29 Metropolitan Museum of Art
10 Martin Luther King, Jr Memorial		30 Gateway Arch
11 9/11 Memorial		

Abb. © Fandorina Liza – Shutterstock.com

Abb. © netsign33 – Shutterstock.com

Abb. © K.Sorokin – Shutterstock.com

Cities and Sights

⭐ Creating a game (2/2)

3. Create: As a group, think about how you could include these sights into your game. Then, design your game either on paper or create it digitally. Use the Task Attack steps to plan your work.

Checklist – Attack the task:
- ⃝ Decide as a group what exactly you want to do.
- ⃝ Think about the steps you have to take in order to reach your goal.
- ⃝ Split up the different steps into smaller tasks.
- ⃝ Assign each team member with different tasks.
- ⃝ Set a time frame and a schedule for the different tasks to be completed on time.

Your game has to fulfill the following criteria:

Checklist – Criteria:
- ⃝ suitable for at least 4 players
- ⃝ includes activities to do
- ⃝ includes questions to answer
- ⃝ includes detailed rules on how to play
- ⃝ includes at least 4 different sights

Cities and Sights

More creativity

⭐ A new Lady Liberty (1/2)

The Lady Liberty is probably one of the most famous and popular sights in the USA. She was a gift from France to celebrate 100 years of U.S. **independence** in 1886. Meant as a symbol for the **desire** for freedom and the **abolishment** of slavery, she became a symbol for so much more: As the first thing that millions of immigrants saw when they came to the USA, she soon became a symbol for the hopes and chances that would **await** the people looking for a better life.

The poem "The New Colossus" can be found on a **plaque** on the **pedestal** of the statue and talks about the Statue of Liberty as a woman welcoming the immigrants looking for a better life in the USA. It was written by Emma Lazarus in 1883.

1. Research: Look up the complete poem. How does it make you feel?

Illustration: Anja Boretzki

 A symbol packed with meaning
Why does the "Liberty **Enlightening** the World" – which is her official name – look the way she does?
Lady Liberty's face is said to **be sculpted** after the artist's mother. The rest of the design is packed with meaning. Let's look at some of them: On her head she is wearing a crown with seven **spikes**. They symbolize rays of light and also the seven seas and continents.
The **torch** in her hand lights the way to freedom.
At her feet you can see broken **shackles** – a symbol meant to represent the end of slavery. But in 1886, freedom was not a reality for African-American people. Racism and discrimination went on.
The Statue of Liberty was therefore just the beginning of a long road towards **equality**, liberty and justice for all.

> **independence:** die Unabhängigkeit, **desire:** die Sehnsucht, **abolishment:** die Abschaffung, **to await:** erwarten, **plaque:** die Tafel, **pedestal:** das Podest, **to enlighten:** erleuchten, aufklären, **to sculpt:** formen, **spike:** die Zacke, **torch:** die Fackel, **shackle:** die Fessel, **equality:** die Gleichberechtigung

Cities and Sights

⭐ A new Lady Liberty (2/2)

2. Create: Design a modern Lady Liberty. Here are some things to think about when you design your sculpture:

- ☆ Which cause is important to you?
- ☆ Whose face should your statue be sculpted after? Which person today stands for the fight for a good cause? Which cause is it?
- ☆ Think of at least one of the "old" Lady Liberty's symbols that you can replace with a more modern symbol. Which symbol do you choose? What does the symbol stand for?
- ☆ Which words would you write onto the pedestal? Why?
- ☆ Where would be the best place for you to put your statue? Why?
- ☆ What name would you give your statue? Why?

3. Present: Present your ideas to the class.

Cities and Sights

More creativity

⭐ Creative Task Assessment Scale

Name: ....

	Criteria	0	1	2	3
1	You did extensive research and found the most relevant information.				
2	You developed your own ideas and included them in your final result.				
3	In your team, you played fair and supported each other.				
4	You included all your team members' ideas into your final result.				
5	When you weren't on the same page, you focused on solving the problem quickly and fairly.				
6	You presented your final result in an engaging way.				
7	Your ideas in the final result are logically structured.				
8	(Optional) Your final result meets the criteria specified on the worksheet.				
				TOTAL	............../..............

From History to Stories

What is this chapter about?

Geschichte lässt sich nicht so einfach schreiben. Geschichte besteht immer aus individuellen Geschichten, aus verschiedenen Wahrheiten. Geschichte wurde nie losgelöst vom eigenen Weltbild, den Vorstellungen von sich selbst und anderen und den eigenen Werten aufgeschrieben. Vielleicht ist dies vor allem auch wahr für die Geschichtsschreibung der USA: eine Geschichtsschreibung, die vor allem *weiß*[3] und männlich ist. Viele Geschichten wurden viel zu lange nicht gehört – denn erzählt wurden sie durchaus. Und so ist die Geschichte der USA, wie wir sie bisweilen wahrnehmen, vor allem eine Geschichte, wie sie der *weiße* Mann erzählt. Umso wichtiger, dass wir auch unseren Lernenden – bei aller didaktischer Reduktion und in dem Wissen, dass wir niemals „alles" erzählen können – einen breiteren Horizont vermitteln.

Für dieses Kapitel habe ich mich ganz bewusst dagegen entschieden, den Lernenden „Geschichte" näherbringen zu wollen. Vielmehr hoffe ich, dass sie durch die Beschäftigung mit verschiedenen exemplarischen Geschichten zu der Erkenntnis kommen, dass die USA viel mehr ist als das Land, das Kolumbus einst eroberte und das *weiße* Männer vermeintlich erst zu dem machten, was es heute ist. Denn die Geschichten, die hinter diesem Land stecken, sind viel vielfältiger und aufregender – wir müssen nur lernen, zuzuhören.

In diesem Kapitel werden verschiedene „stories" erzählt: Die uns bekannten Geschichten werden durch die Geschichten von Schwarzen Menschen, People of Color, Frauen und Natives erweitert.

Bei allen Bemühungen und aller Umsicht, die ich versucht habe, walten zu lassen, ist mir bewusst, dass eine didaktische Reduktion oder auch Verkürzung – so gut gemeint sie auch sein mag – Menschen verletzen kann. Auch darauf sollten wir im Umgang mit unseren Lernenden immer wieder hinweisen. „Richtig" kann man es nur im Einzelfall machen, wenn man sich offen und auf Augenhöhe begegnet.

An jede „story" schließt sich eine kreative Aufgabe an. Am Ende des Kapitels findet sich keine umfangreiche mix-and-match-Aufgabensammlung, da diese der Vielfalt und all den verschiedenen Blickwinkeln nur schwer gerecht werden könnte. Stattdessen habe ich mich für eine Aufgabe entschieden, die die Lernenden dazu einladen soll, sich kreativ und gestalterisch mit der Vielfalt der amerikanischen Geschichten auseinanderzusetzen.

---

[3] Die Adjektive werden hier bewusst einmal kursiv, einmal großgeschrieben, um zu verdeutlichen, dass es nicht um Farben geht. Die Schreibweise soll verdeutlichen, dass die damit beschriebenen Menschen aufgrund ihrer Hautfarbe unterschiedlich privilegiert sind und unterschiedliche Lebensrealitäten haben.

From History to Stories

Pocahontas and the early colonists

Pocahontas was the youngest daughter of the leader of the Powhatan people, Wahunsenaca. She was about 10 or 11 years old when the English arrived on the East Coast in 1607. The **tribe** decided not to fight them but to make them **allies**. Wahunsenaca sent them food and often his daughter was allowed to go on these trips.

 Powhatan was an **alliance** of at least 30 tribes that lived in the area that is known as Virginia today. They grew **corn** and other **crops** and went hunting and fishing.

The English put up a settlement they called Jamestown. When the colonists grew hungry, they demanded more and more food from the Natives, using weapons and violence. They **wiped out** complete villages to take the land and **enslaved** the inhabitants. Wahunsenaca didn't allow his daughter to go to the English anymore.

When Pocahontas grew older, she married Kocoum and they had a child together. There had been **rumors** that the English were planning on kidnapping Pocahontas, so she went to live in a small village with her husband's family. But hiding didn't help: The English kidnapped Pocahontas, put her on a ship and killed her husband. She was put into English clothes and had to become a Christian. She became deeply depressed and experienced a mental breakdown. The English sent for support from a sister and so her oldest sister Mattachanna and her husband came to live with her.

Pocahontas had to marry John Rolfe, an Englishman who wanted to make money growing tobacco, but hadn't succeeded so far. After the two were married, the Powhatan agreed to share their knowledge with him: Suddenly, his business was successful.

In 1616, Pocahontas and some other Powhatans were taken to a tour through England. There had been rumors that the English planned to murder Pocahontas, but she had no other choice but to go with them in order to protect her people. The colonists wanted to show the people in the old world that their **settlement** was a success: "The Natives and us are friends!" and "We grow the best tobacco!" On the journey home, in spring 1617, Pocahontas – who had been in best health before – suddenly fell sick and died.

---

tribe: der Volksstamm, **ally:** der/die Verbündete, **alliance:** das Bündnis, **corn:** der Mais, **crop:** die Nutzpflanze, **to wipe out sth.:** etw. auslöschen, **to enslave:** versklaven, **rumor:** das Gerücht, **settlement:** die Siedlung

From History to Stories

Pocahontas and the early colonists

★ Designing a storytelling gourd

The Powhatan use **gourds** as **containers**, for example for water. And they have also used them as objects of art for centuries until today. The paintings on the gourds tell the tribe's story.

1. Create: Design a gourd telling Pocahontas' story. You can either choose a single event or try to include more events in your design.

2. Present: Tell your class about the event(s) you chose using your gourd.

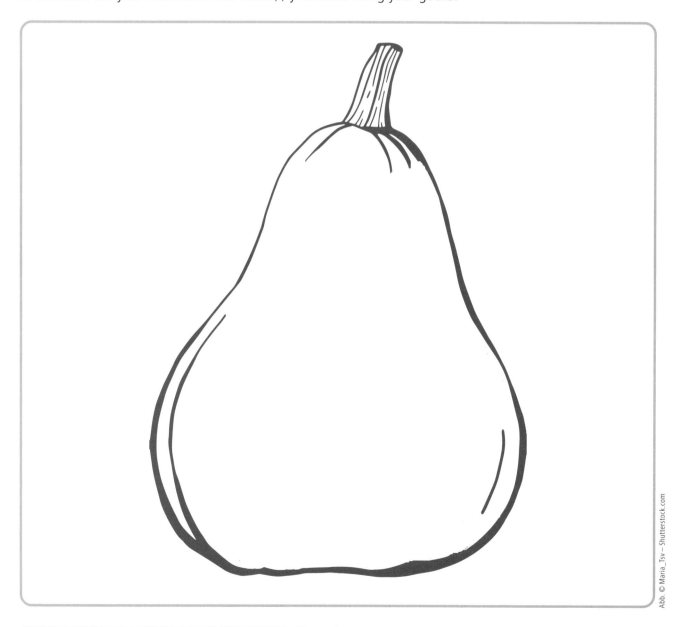

gourd: der Flaschenkürbis, **container:** der Transportbehälter

From History to Stories

Sitting Bull: a fighter for his people

Born as the son of a chief of the Hunkpapa Lakota, Sitting Bull grew into a **skilled** buffalo hunter, who proved to be a great **warrior**, too. In 1868, he became chief, making him **responsible for** the **well-being** of his people. He is remembered for never giving up and never stopping to fight for his people.

 During the 19th century, more and more people were moving west. Some of them were **miners** who wanted to get rich during the Gold Rush. Others were **settlers**: The Homestead Act of 1862 promised 160 acres of land to any man who agreed to farm it for five years. Thousands took this opportunity. However, most of the land already belonged to various **tribes** and nations of Natives. The white people showed no respect for them: They took their land and **wiped out** complete herds of buffalo.

Sitting Bull

Little Bighorn

Sitting Bull and other chiefs didn't want to sell their holy land to the white settlers – so the whites decided to **force** them to leave. Sitting Bull was convinced that they could win against the white people if they fought together. On June 25, 1876, it all came down to the Battle of Little Bighorn. The U.S. Army officers had come to bring a village of Natives under their control. The Natives **surrounded** them and won. In return, the government sent thousands of troops, burned down Native villages and forced the tribes to move to reservations. Sitting Bull still didn't **give in** and led 2,000 people to Canada.

Back in the USA

In Canada, it was hard for them to find enough buffalo to provide food. People began going back to the reservations in the United States. Eventually, Sitting Bull went with his people. There officials came to **arrest** him because they feared he could lead an **uprising** among his people. On December 15, 1890, he was shot during the arrest.

---

skilled: fähig, **warrior**: der Krieger/die Kriegerin, **to be responsible for sth.**: für etw. verantwortlich sein, **well-being**: das Wohlergehen, **miner**: der Minenarbeiter/die Minenarbeiterin, **settler**: der Siedler/die Siedlerin, **tribe**: der Volksstamm, **to wipe out sth.**: etw. auslöschen, **to force sb.**: jmd. zwingen, **to surround**: umzingeln, **to give in**: nachgeben, **to arrest sb.**: jmd. verhaften, **uprising**: der Aufstand

From History to Stories

Sitting Bull: a fighter for his people

⭐ Creating a name

When a child was born in the Sioux nation, they were given a name that would mostly last through childhood. Whenever something happened in the life of a person that changed them or had a big impact on them, their names could change.

For example: Sitting Bull was given the name "Jumping Badger" when he was born. But when he was a child, he was very quiet: He looked at things carefully before grabbing them and he always thought carefully before answering a question. Jumping Badger was now called "Slow" instead. Having proven to be a great hunter and warrior, his father gave him his own name "Sitting Bull" which stood for strength and courage.

1. Together: Ask your friends and family which name they would give you today. Which animals fits your character and outlook on life or even your appearance?

2. Write: Think of one adjective that best describes you. The word boxes might help you to come up with some ideas. Look up the meaning of the words if you don't know them already.

Animals	adjectives
squirrel, beaver, bison, bear, raccoon, bobcat, bullfrog, alligator, eagle, cougar, jaguar, owl, robin, shark, snake …	adventurous, nice, calm, caring, creative, funny, wise, shy, smart, ambitious, artistic, easy-going, kind, laid-back, clever, fair, loyal, quiet, cheerful …

3. Write: Complete the sentences below.

The animal that reminds others of me is .... because ....

I think the best thing about this animal is ....

One adjective that describes me really well is ....

I show this trait when ....

The name I choose for my life today is ....

From History to Stories

Education for extinction

In 1819, U.S. Congress passed the so-called "Indian Civilization Act". Thousands of dollars were spent on building **boarding schools** for children of Native Americans far away from the reservations. Indigenous children were often taken from their families **by force**. Families tried to avoid this by hiding their children or pretending they were not Natives.

The government thought that separating children from their families and their culture was the only way for them to get a "**decent** education", i.e. to learn how to read and write. Their real goal, however, was for Native culture to **go extinct**. They wanted them to fully take on the dominant European American, white culture.

At school, officials cut the children's hair, gave them other names, took away their traditional clothing and put them into uniforms. The children had to give up their languages and cultural traditions. They were trained to do jobs in the industry, as **farmhands**, **carpenters** or **domestic servants**.

Passed-down trauma

After being taken away from their families, the children were told over and over again that being a Native American was bad. **Physical punishment** and **sexual abuse** of both boys and girls was widespread in boarding schools. Children were too far from home to turn to their parents for help. Some ran away, some died trying. Some continued their traditions in secret.

This **harsh** treatment deeply traumatized them for the rest of their lives. Added to this were feelings of shame and powerlessness from historical losses of land, family and culture. This abuse often led to bad treatment of their own children. In a cycle of violence, the hurt was **passed down** from one generation to the next, having traumatic **long-term** effects on the whole community up until today.

---

extinction: die Ausrottung, **boarding school:** das Internat, **by force:** mit Gewalt, **decent:** anständig, **to go extinct:** aussterben, **farmhand:** der Landarbeiter/die Landarbeiterin, **carpenter:** der Zimmermann/die Zimmerin, **domestic servant:** der Hausdiener/die Hausdienerin, **physical punishment:** die körperliche Bestrafung, **sexual abuse:** die sexualisierte Gewalt, **harsh:** brutal, **to pass down:** weitergeben, **long-term:** Langzeit-

From History to Stories

Education for extinction

⭐ What's your story? Pack a box!

Storytelling has always been an important part of Native American cultures. People shared their own stories as well as their **tribes**' ones. The stories have helped to keep their cultures and identities alive.

What is your life's story? What defines you? What makes you you?

1. Create: Pack a box with all different kinds of things that tell a story about you, your past, your present and your future. You can use an old shoebox, for example. Add things, pictures, texts and interactive **foldable** elements.

The following questions can help you come up with ideas:

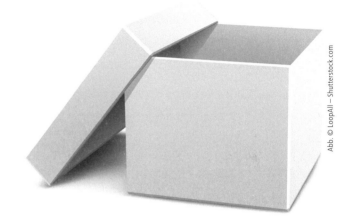

- ☆ Which culture do you see yourself belonging to?
- ☆ What role does your family's history play in the way you live? Which special days are important? Which traditions are important for your family and yourself?
- ☆ What are beautiful childhood memories of yours? What made you happy when you were little?
- ☆ What are your hobbies? What makes you happy now?
- ☆ What are your life goals? What will make you happy in the future?
- ☆ What are your **values**? What is important to you? Which people matter to you the most?

2. Present: Display your boxes in the classroom. Have a look at your classmates' boxes.

3. Discuss: Talk about your boxes: Is there anything new and interesting you found out about your classmates? Are there any questions you would like to ask your classmates?

---

tribe: der Volksstamm, **foldable:** faltbar, **value:** der Wert

From History to Stories

Standing up at Standing Rock

> On March 25, 2020 Mike Faith, Standing Rock Sioux Tribe Chairman, said: "After years of **commitment** to **defending** our water and earth, we welcome this news of a **significant** **legal** win."⁴

What had happened?

In July 2014, a company called Energy Transfer Partners **announced** the building of an underground **pipeline** that should bring **crude oil** from North Dakota all the way to Illinois. It was to run through Standing Rock reservation, extremely close to the Missouri river and under Lake Oahe.

In September 2016, the tribe set up a camp of protesters (calling themselves "protectors"), including members from other **tribes** and environmental activists. Their position was this:
- ☆ The land is **sacred** for them. You can find **burial grounds** of their **ancestors** there.
- ☆ They want to protect their water, which they need for agriculture, drinking and religious use. They are afraid of **leaks** that would **poison** the water.

The violence against the protesters escalated quickly: **water cannons**, **tear gas**, **rubber bullets** and dogs were used, resulting in the injury of men, women and even children. In November 2016, President Obama said that a new route would be **reviewed**.

But then came Donald Trump. Shortly after he became president in January 2017, he decided that the pipeline should be built as soon as possible – without a new review. In May 2017, the first oil was delivered through the pipeline. But the legal fight went on – even after the protesters had left the camp. In 2020 and 2021, several **courts** – including the U.S. Supreme Court – sided with the Standing Rock Sioux. They all agreed that the review had not been **sufficient** – meaning that officials should never have allowed the pipeline to be built on this route.

---

commitment: der Einsatz, **to defend:** verteidigen, **significant:** bedeutsam, **legal:** rechtlich, **to announce:** ankündigen, **pipeline:** die Rohrleitung, **crude oil:** das Rohöl, **tribe:** der Volksstamm; **sacred:** heilig, **burial ground:** das Gräberfeld, **ancestor:** der Vorfahre/die Vorfahrin, **leak:** das Leck, **to poison:** vergiften, **water cannon:** der Wasserwerfer, **tear gas:** das Tränengas, **rubber bullet:** das Gummigeschoss, **to review:** überprüfen, **court:** das Gericht, **sufficient:** ausreichend

---

⁴ Quote from: https://www.theguardian.com/us-news/2020/mar/25/dakota-access-pipeline-permits-court-standing-rock, last accessed March 25, 2024.

From History to Stories

Standing up at Standing Rock

⭐ Writing a story book

1. Together: Get together in groups. Make up a character who might have been part of the protests. This could be a **tribal elder**, a young activist, or even a friendly animal looking at what is happening.

2. Research: Find out more about the protests and the camp at Standing Rock. Look specifically at pictures, try to get the basic idea and think about emotions involved.

3. Think: Brainstorm a simple story that involves your character and gives details about the protests. Make sure to include the **challenges** of the protests, feelings and lessons that your character might experience. Only write down keywords.

4. Create: Illustrate your story. You can work digitally or by hand, using all kinds of different art tools. Show scenes from your story, include your character, other people and the natural environment. Decide if you want to use **spreads**, single pages, or a mix of both.

5. Write: Write only short sentences or **captions** for each page of your story book. Describe the events and include important messages that you learned about while doing your research.
Put the story books together. Find a title for your story book. Design a cover with the title and the authors' and illustrators' names.

6. Present: Display the story books in your classroom or share them with other students.
Talk about which story books you enjoyed most. Which ones convey the message of Standing Rock best? Which ones are illustrated best? Which main character do you find most interesting?

---

tribal elder: der/die Stammesälteste, **challenge:** die Herausforderung, **spread:** die Doppelseite, **caption:** die Bildunterschrift

From History to Stories

George Washington and the American Revolution

George Washington

In 1754, France and Britain both wanted to **gain** more land east of the Mississippi River. Both sides were supported by Native **tribes**. One night in May, a group of British soldiers and Ohio Iroquois soldiers attacked a French camp. The leader of the British soldiers was George Washington, he was only 22 years old and had never been in **combat** before. This fight escalated quickly into a bigger conflict: the French and Indian War which would lead to a World War only two years later.

 After the Seven Years' War, the British government was in debt. So they **imposed** **taxes** on the colonies to pay for the war. The colonists in the first 13 colonies thought that this was unfair: They should pay taxes, but didn't have a **representative** in the British Parliament. This meant they had no say on taxes or the laws that were imposed on the colonies.

Washington was named commander-in-chief for the Continental Army, fighting against the British in the Revolutionary War which started in 1775. In 1776, the Continental Congress published a document in which they explained why the thirteen colonies were **declaring** their **independence**. The Revolutionary War went on for eight long years. In the end, the colonists won with the help of the French. Washington became a national hero. When Britain accepted the USA as an independent state, Washington gave up his military career – thinking he had done everything he could – and wanted nothing more than a quiet life.

In 1787, he was asked to help manage the team writing the new constitution. He impressed people so much that they wanted him to run for president. Washington **hesitated** at first but then **gave in**: After the **election** in January, he became the first president of the USA in April 1789.

> **to gain**: gewinnen, **tribe**: der Volksstamm, **combat**: das Gefecht, **to impose**: etw. erheben, **tax**: die Steuer, **representative**: der Vertreter/die Vertreterin, **to declare**: erklären, verkünden, **independence**: die Unabhängigkeit, **to hesitate**: zögern, **to give in**: nachgeben, **election**: die Wahl

From History to Stories

George Washington and the American Revolution

⭐ Having a debate

1. Research: In 1773, the Boston Tea Party took place. It was a major **incident** of the American Revolution. Find the answers to the following questions:
- ☆ What was the reason for the Boston Tea Party? What happened?
- ☆ Who organized it? Who were the key figures?
- ☆ What were the perspectives of the Patriots (**affirmative** group) and the Loyalists (**opposing** group)?

2. Together: Split the class into two groups: the Patriots' side and the Loyalists' side. Then, divide the two main groups into smaller ones: get together in groups of 3 students.

3. Think: Come up with arguments for or against the taxation on tea. Use historical facts. Think about which arguments the other side could come up with and how you could react to them. Practice giving them.

4. Debate: One team will be the Patriots, one will be the Loyalists. The rest of the class will judge the quality of the arguments and the performance in the debate.
- ☆ The first speaker of the affirmative team presents an opening statement. (3–5 minutes)
- ☆ The first speaker of the opposing team gives an opening statement. (3–5 minutes)
- ☆ The second speaker of the affirmative team adds more arguments to support their perspective. (3–5 minutes)
- ☆ The second speaker of the opposing team presents further arguments. (3–5 minutes)
- ☆ Time for the preparation of the **rebuttals**. Don't add new information. Defend your perspective and try to defeat the other side's arguments. (5 minutes)
- ☆ The third speaker of the opposing team begins with the rebuttal. (3–5 minutes)
- ☆ The third speaker of the affirmative team gives the rebuttal. (3–5 minutes)
- ☆ The opposing team gives their closing statement. Do not add new information. Summarize your ideas. (3–5 minutes)
- ☆ The affirmative team gives their closing statement. Do not add new information. Summarize your ideas. (3–5 minutes)

5. Discuss: Which side was more convincing? Who had the best arguments? Who played their role best? How did you feel giving your statements?

> **incident:** der Vorfall, **affirmative:** zustimmend, **opposing:** Gegen-, **rebuttal:** die Widerlegung

From History to Stories

From miners to millions: the story of Levi Strauss

Levi Strauss was born in 1829 as Löb Strauss in a small village near Bamberg, Germany. The family was poor and Löb's two older brothers went to find a better life in the USA. Two years after their father had died, Löb and his sisters **emigrated** to New York, too. His two older brothers owned a store that sold things needed for **sewing** (like buttons and **fabric**) in New York. There, he began to learn the **trade** himself. He also changed his name into something more American: Löb became Levi.

 When gold was found in a **mine** in California in 1848, the Gold Rush soon led thousands of people west. The largest migration in American history began.

Going West

When Levi heard the news of the Gold Rush, he moved to San Francisco. But he was not up to finding gold himself. He opened a business as the West Coast **counterpart** of his family's store in New York. He called it: Levi Strauss and Co.

A brilliant idea

One of Levi's customers had an idea: Jacob Davis, a **tailor** from Nevada, had found a way to make the pants of his customers **last** longer by adding **rivets** at certain points. Davis needed a business partner to raise the money to **patent** this new idea. Levi was all in! In 1873, the patent **was granted** and the blue jeans were born: a **garment** so solid that even horses can't rip them apart.

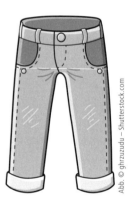

Becoming a fashion icon

The blue jeans were first called "XX men's overalls" and were mostly worn by miners. But that wasn't the end of the story. The blue jeans are probably the most famous piece of clothing around the world, being worn in all kinds of different styles.

> **to emigrate:** auswandern, **to sew:** nähen, **fabric:** der Stoff, **trade:** das Handwerk, **mine:** die Mine, **counterpart:** das Gegenstück, **tailor:** der Schneider/die Schneiderin, **to last:** halten, Bestand haben, **rivet:** die Niete, **to patent:** patentieren, **to be granted:** etw. gewährt bekommen, **garment:** das Kleidungsstück

From History to Stories

From miners to millions: the story of Levi Strauss

⭐ Adventure Board Game

1. Research: Find out more about the Gold Rush. These questions can help you:
- ☆ Where was the gold found?
- ☆ Where did the miners come from?
- ☆ Which **impact** did it have on **society**?
- ☆ And which **challenges** came with it – for miners, settlers and Natives?

2. Together: Get together in small groups. Create a board game about the Gold Rush. Include key elements like mining for gold, traveling through dangerous **terrain** and living in a **boom town**.

> **Checklist:**
> - ◯ Create a game board and game cards.
> - ◯ **Craft tokens**.
> - ◯ Add questions about the Gold Rush that the players have to answer.
> - ◯ Think of a set of rules that are clear and fair.
> - ◯ Have another group of students play your game and give feedback.
> - ◯ Use the feedback to make your game even better.

3. Present: Present your game to the class. Explain the history behind your game and how your game shows the challenges and the lifestyle of the era.

4. Reflect: Talk about what you have learned through this project.

---

impact: der Einfluss, **society:** die Gesellschaft, **challenge:** die Herausforderung, **terrain:** das Gebiet, **boom town:** eine Stadt, die in kürzester Zeit einen wirtschaftlichen Aufschwung erlebt, **to craft:** bauen, basteln, **token:** der Spielstein

From History to Stories

Honest Abe's quest for unity

Abraham Lincoln

When Abraham Lincoln was a young man, he started to work as a **sales clerk** in a store in Illinois. That's when he first earned his nickname "**Honest** Abe". Legend has it that he would close the shop and run after a client when he realized that he had **shortchanged** them – even if it was just a few pennies. People soon respected him for his honesty and turned to him as a **mediator** or judge – both fields in which he further proved to be an honest person.

In 1860, Lincoln **ran for** president. He was known to be against **enslavement** and, therefore, soon after his election seven states left the union. Lincoln decided to fight for the unity of the USA. A war was about to shake the United States to the core.

> **Raging** from 1861 to 1865, the Civil War was the deadliest war in American history: more than 620,000 lives were lost. It was fought between the Northern (Union) and the Southern states (Confederates). The Confederates separated from the United States to form their own government. There were several reasons for the Civil War, but one **crucial** point was this: Southern states **relied on** enslavement for their **agricultural** production and didn't want to lose this source of labor. Many Northern states, on the other hand, were **abolitionist**.

In 1863, Lincoln signed the Emancipation Proclamation: an official statement that marked an important step to ending enslavement. On April 9, 1865, the Confederates' most important army **surrendered** to the Union. Shortly after, the South's other armies also lay down their weapons. The unity of all states was within reach again. But Lincoln would not live to see what he had fought for: He was shot while visiting a play at Ford's Theater in Washington by Confederate sympathizer John Wilkes Boothe.
On December 6, 1865 the Thirteenth Amendment, an addition to the U.S. Constitution, made enslavement illegal in the entire United States.

---

unity: die Einheit, **sales clerk:** der Verkäufer/die Verkäuferin, **honest:** ehrlich,
to shortchange: zu wenig Rückgeld geben, **mediator:** der Schlichter/die Schlichterin,
to run for: für etw. kandidieren, **enslavement:** die Versklavung, **to rage:** wüten,
crucial: entscheidend, **to rely on sth.:** auf etw. angewiesen sein, **agricultural:** landwirtschaftlich, **abolitionist:** eine Person, die die Versklavung abschaffen will,
to surrender: sich ergeben

From History to Stories

Honest Abe's quest for unity

⭐ **Writing a journal**

1. Research: Find out about Abraham Lincoln's early life, from his birth to the 1830s. Focus on his experiences and **values** that are related to honesty. Think about which key moments **shaped** his character. Use the lines below to take notes.

2. Create: Write journal entries about Lincoln's life. Imagine you were young Lincoln and you were living his life at that time. You can either use pens and paper or you can choose to work digitally.

☆ **Include honesty:** Document at least three key moments in which Lincoln showed honesty. These could be real events or you could also make up scenarios based on his values.

☆ **Reflect:** At the end of each scenario include the answers to the following questions:
  ▷ Why was it important for Abraham Lincoln to show honesty at this point?
  ▷ What were the consequences of his honesty?
  ▷ How did it make him feel?

☆ **Illustrate:** Use drawings and illustrations to go with each journal entry.

3. Present: Share parts of your journal with your class. Which stories did you like most? Talk about if and when honesty is important and which impact it has on others.

....

....

....

....

....

....

....

....

journal: das Tagebuch, **value:** der Wert, **to shape:** formen

From History to Stories

Harriet Tubman: a guiding light to freedom

Harriet Tubman was born sometime between 1820 and 1822. Because her parents weren't free, she was **enslaved** at birth. Unfortunately, we don't know Harriet Tubman's exact date of birth because slave owners didn't think it was important to record the births of the children of their enslaved workers. Before she was 6, she was **rented out** to different neighbours: She had to leave her family and work as a **domestic servant**.

Harriet Tubman

> The transatlantic slave trade began when the colonies on the American continent needed workers. People **were shipped** from Africa to the Americas like **cargo**. Then they were **forced** to work on plantations or in homes and shops. They were treated like **property** and weren't allowed to learn to read or write. In the 18th and 19th century, more and more people were thinking that slavery should end: They were called abolitionists. In 1865, enslavement was finally **abolished**.

When she was twelve, Harriet Tubman was hit on the head with a two-pound weight when she tried to help a man who was **escaping** from a farm: She had bad headaches and is suspected to have experienced **narcolepsy** for the rest of her life. In 1849, she escaped to Philadelphia. Again and again, she took trips to Maryland to help others escape. She carried a gun to defend against slave catchers and risked her own life every time. She managed to guide 50 to 70 people to freedom.

> The Underground Railroad was a secret network that helped enslaved people escape into freedom. It was made up of brave individuals: sailors who hid people on ships leaving the Southern ports, people offering safe places to stay, abolitionists in the North who helped with food, money and helped **in court**. Most helpers were free Black people or those who had escaped enslavement themselves.

---

enslaved: versklavt, **to rent sth./sb. out:** etw./jmd. vermieten, **domestic servant:** der Hausdiener/die Hausdienerin, **to be shipped:** verschifft werden, **cargo:** die Fracht, **to force sb.:** jmd. zwingen, **property:** das Eigentum, **to be abolished:** abgeschafft werden, **to escape:** entkommen, **narcolepsy:** die Narkolepsie, plötzliches krankhaftes Einschlafen, **in court:** vor Gericht

From History to Stories

Harriet Tubman: a guiding light to freedom

⭐ The Underground Railroad

The Underground Railroad wasn't a real railroad, but a movement to resist **enslavement** through **escape**. Just like trains that move underground and can't be seen, this "railroad" led people to safety in secret. People who fled enslavement during these times are today referred to as "freedom seekers". People who were willing to help them are called "**conductors**".

1. Research:
- ☆ Research the routes of the Underground Railroad: Where did they start? Where did they lead? How did geography influence the routes?
- ☆ Get to know the conductors: Find out about key figures involved in the Underground Railroad. Who were the conductors? What motivated them to take on the risks?
- ☆ Explore safe houses: Which locations provided **shelter** for the freedom seekers? What were these locations like? How did they manage to remain secret?
- ☆ Decode the symbols: People on the Underground Railroad network used codes and symbols to communicate. Find out about their meaning and how they were used.
- ☆ Uncover brave stories: Find out about personal stories of people on the Underground Railroad. What challenges and problems did they find on their way?

2. Create: You can create a poster or a digital presentation. Make sure to include maps, pictures and **first-person narratives**.

3. Present: Present your findings to the class.

4. Reflect and discuss: What did you feel like while doing your research? What do the stories teach us about the importance of equality and human rights?

> **enslavement:** die Versklavung, **escape:** das Entkommen, **conductor:** der Schaffner/die Schaffnerin, **shelter:** die Zuflucht, **first-person narrative:** Erzählung aus der Ich-Perspektive

From History to Stories

"No." – How Rosa Parks took a stand for justice

Rosa Parks

It was an evening in early December 1955 in Montgomery, Alabama. Rosa Parks was sitting in the so-called "colored section" of the bus. The white people were sitting in the "white section". When more and more white people got on the bus, the Black people **were required** to get up and give their seats to them.

But Rosa Parks was tired – not only because it had been a long day at work but also tired of the **injustice** that Black people had to face every day. Her grandfather was born enslaved and had taught her that is was unfair how differently Black people were treated. She and her husband had joined the "National **Association** for the **Advancement** of Colored People" (NAACP), working towards ending discrimination and **segregation**. So this time she didn't get up. She stood up for what was right by sitting down. Her "No!" **echoed** through the land and sparked a series of events that made Rosa Parks "the mother of the civil rights movement".

 At that time, Southern states of the USA operated under the Jim Crow laws. These laws claimed to give African Americans "separate but equal" rights. Their main goal, however, was to keep Black and white **citizens** as far apart as possible. Children didn't go to the same schools, there were separate restaurants, toilets and waiting rooms. Blacks were kept from taking higher-paying jobs and it was made very hard for them to **vote**.

The Montgomery Bus Boycott

When Rosa Parks **was arrested** for her behavior on that bus, Black citizens in Montgomery stopped using buses. That meant that they had to walk far because only a few owned cars, or that they had to **carpool**. Still, they kept up the boycott for more than a year. This hit the city's transport services hard, because African Americans made up more than 70 % of the bus users and so the services missed out on a lot of money. Finally, the Supreme Court stated that Alabama's segregation laws were against the Constitution. What a **victory**!

> **to be required to do sth.:** etw. tun müssen, **injustice:** die Ungerechtigkeit, **association:** die Gesellschaft, der Verein, **advancement:** der Fortschritt, **segregation:** die (sogenannte) Rassentrennung, **to echo:** schallen, **citizen:** der Bürger/die Bürgerin, **to vote:** wählen, **to be arrested:** in Haft genommen werden, **to carpool:** eine Fahrgemeinschaft bilden, **victory:** der Sieg

From History to Stories

"No." – How Rosa Parks took a stand for justice

★ The Civil Rights Movement: peaceful protest

 In 1963, about 250,000 people took part in the March on Washington, a protest focused on civil rights and ending segregation. Some speakers were famous musicians or actors and actresses. But the highlight was when Martin Luther King, Jr. went up to the podium, giving his famous "I Have a Dream" speech. The march made people aware of the Civil Rights Movement and helped start a more equal and fair life for all.

1. Think: Which injustices do you think are most important to fight against today? Which injustices would you stand up against?

2. Create: Fill the picture below with life.
Add faces to the drawing. Show people's emotions and actions: Are they happy? Determined? Mad? Angry? Are they quiet or shouting?
Add words to the posters: What do these people want to change most?

3. Present: Use the sentences below to explain your main ideas.

Today we should protest for / against … .
People feel … because …
My dream for a better world is …

We all should …
I think it's important that we …

From History to Stories

Celebrating excellence: the Obamas' footprint

Their time in the White House marked a **pivotal moment** in the history of the USA: a power couple that inspired young and old.

 All people are **equal** and have the same rights and chances? What a great idea, but unfortunately this is not true for so many people. As a result of ongoing discrimination, Black people today still don't have the same chances when it comes to building **wealth**, getting a higher education and reaching positions of power.

Barack and Michelle Obama

Barack and Michelle

When Barack Obama became the 44th president of the U.S., he brought hope for many Black citizens: he was the first African American president ever, coming from a middle-class family. He showed that anyone could reach high positions – no matter what background they came from.

His wife Michelle gave her all during the time as a First Lady. Just like Barack she **had studied law** and wanted to encourage students – especially those from **disadvantaged** backgrounds – to go for higher education. Barack and Michelle soon became role models and sources of inspiration that dreams can **be achieved** through hard work, **determination** and education.

Their **legacy**

The Obama **administration** and the couple themselves helped create a more equal **society**: for example, the number of People of Color finishing high school went up. Barack Obama also made it an important part of his agenda to make sure that women get paid the same as men when doing the same work. This is a huge step against discrimination in general.

> **pivotal moment:** entscheidender Moment, **equal:** gleich, **wealth:** der Wohlstand, **to study law:** Jura studieren, **disadvantaged:** benachteiligt, **to be achieved:** erreicht werden, **determination:** die Entschlossenheit, **legacy:** das Vermächtnis, das Erbe, **administration:** die Regierung, **society:** die Gesellschaft

From History to Stories

Celebrating excellence: The Obamas' footprint

⭐ Creating a vision board

1. Think: What inspires you? Where do you see yourself in the future? What are your goals for the next year, the next five years or even your life? Choose one role model for your vision board as well. You can use the space below to brainstorm your ideas.

2. Research: Collect information, pictures and materials. Are there any quotes that you can find online that go along with your vision? You might need magazines, postcards, scissors, glue and pens. You could also print pictures.

3. Design: Use a poster or a large sheet of paper as a basis for your vision board. Divide your vision board into different parts: they should represent different aspects of life (for example work, family life, education, community life, etc.)
Start arranging your cut-out pictures and words onto your vision board. Create a collage that represents your own visions for your life.
Add more thoughts. Why are the things on your vision board so important to you?

4. Present: Share your vision board with the rest of the class. Talk about why you chose certain images or quotes.

5. Reflect: Have each student say one sentence about why positive role models are important.

....
....
....
....
....
....
....
....

> **vision**: die Traumvorstellung, die Vision **quote:** das Zitat

From History to Stories

Action for equality: Black Lives Matter

Trayvon Martin was visiting his father in Sanford, Florida. On the evening of February 26, 2012, he went to a store to buy some snacks and then walked back to the house where his dad was staying. The neighborhood **watchman** George Zimmerman saw him, thought that Trayvon **was up to no good** and called the police. Instead of leaving matters to the police, Zimmermann followed him. 17-year-old Trayvon was talking on the phone

On July 20, 2013, protesters carried posters in support of Trayvon Martin and other victims of violence during Comic Con in downtown San Diego, CA.

when he noticed that a man was following him. The police told Zimmerman to stay in his car but he ignored the instructions. Just moments later, neighbors heard gunfire. Arriving at the scene, police found Trayvon Martin shot by George Zimmerman. Zimmerman argued that he had had to shoot the **unarmed** boy in **self-defense**.

 When people are more closely watched by police or other authorities and **are suspected** of a crime based on their looks, it is called racial profiling. Black men are often **affected by** racial profiling because of **stereotypes**. One frequent example for racial profiling is that drivers who are not white **get pulled over** more often than white drivers. These decisions are often rather based on stereotypes than on real **evidence**.

Standing strong together

Trayvon Martin's death in 2012 was just one of several that caused the Black Lives Matter movement. When George Zimmerman **was acquitted** and not charged with murder, people in the USA stood up against discrimination, racism, racial **inequality** and violence against Black people, especially by police. The name "Black Lives Matter" addresses the fact that Black people in the U.S. are far more likely to be killed by police than whites. They want to point out that all lives are **equally** important. The movement has been fighting racism through political action by for example letter-writing campaigns and non-violent protests.

watchman: der Wachmann, **to be up to no good:** nichts Gutes im Sinn haben, **unarmed:** unbewaffnet, **self-defense:** die Selbstverteidigung, **to be suspected:** verdächtigt werden, **to be affected by:** von etw. betroffen sein, **stereotype:** das Vorurteil, **to get pulled over:** (von der Polizei) angehalten werden, **evidence:** der Beweis, **to be acquitted:** freigesprochen werden, **inequality:** die Ungleichheit, **equally:** gleichermaßen

From History to Stories

Action for equality: Black Lives Matter

⭐ Writing a poem

Your task is to write a diamante poem that captures the important points of unity and solidarity within the Black Lives Matter movement.

1. Think: In only two minutes, come up with words and ideas that come to your mind when you think about the Black Lives Matter movement. Write down your thoughts on a separate sheet of paper.

2. Research: Look up some more facts about Black Lives Matter. Only take 10 minutes. Add to your notes.

3. Create: Write your poem.

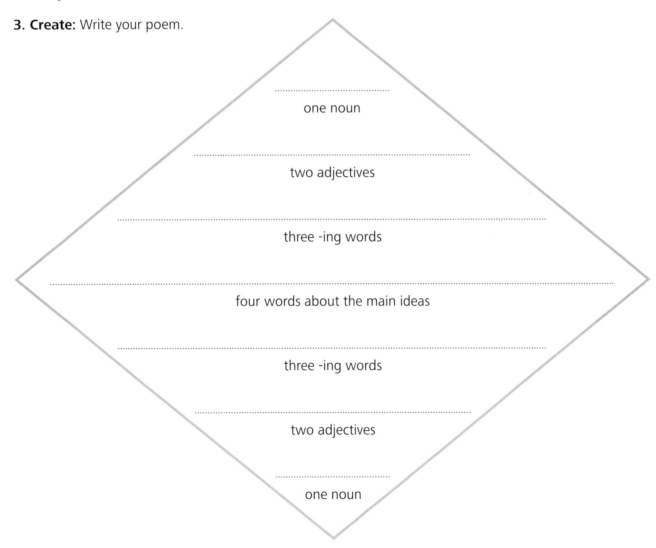

4. Present: Present your poem to the class.

5. Discuss: Talk about which poem your class liked most and why.

From History to Stories

Roselle's remarkable rescue: guiding hope on 9/11

The morning started out like any other: Michael Hingson, who has been blind since birth, started work in his office while his guide dog Roselle was sitting down at his feet. Michael worked for a company located on the 78th floor of the North Tower of the World Trade Center.

Suddenly, they heard a loud boom **rattling** the office, they felt the tower shake. Michael knew they had to get out of there. Roselle **remained calm** as they went to the stairs. The **stairwell** was very crowded and the temperature was rising because of the fire above them. Roselle led Michael and others down 1,435 steps. She was **exhausted** when they reached the ground floor, **panting heavily** and in need of water. She drank from puddles of water created by broken hydrants and led Michael out of the building within minutes. Together they ran to a nearby subway station and made their **escape** – just minutes before the tower **collapsed**.

> On September 11, 2001, 19 terrorists hijacked four airplanes. Two of the planes were flown into the Twin Towers of the World Trade Center in New York City. Both towers collapsed. Another plane flew into the Pentagon near Washington D.C., while the fourth plane crashed in Pennsylvania. Almost 3,000 people died. After the attacks, president George W. Bush started the so-called "War on Terror", including military operations in Afghanistan. Patriotism in the USA increased, making the people stand together in times of this crisis. The events had a global impact, too. For example, airlines all over the world massively tightened their safety **measures**.

The PDSA Dickin Medal

Along with two other dogs, Roselle was awarded the Dickin Medal in 2002. This award is given to animals to **honor** their work in times of war. Roselle's and Salty's (another guide dog in the Twin Towers) citation reads: "For remaining loyally at the side of their blind owners, **courageously** leading them down more than 70 floors of the World Trade Center and to a place of safety following the terrorist attack on New York on 11 September 2001."

> **to rattle:** erschüttern, **to remain:** bleiben, **calm:** ruhig, **stairwell:** das Treppenhaus, **exhausted:** erschöpft, **to pant heavily:** schwer atmen, **escape:** das Entkommen, **to collapse:** zusammenbrechen, **measure:** die Maßnahme, **to honor:** ehren, **courageously:** mutig

From History to Stories

Roselle's remarkable rescue: guiding hope on 9/11

★ The heroes of 9/11: creating a profile

1. Research: Find out about the human heroes of 9/11:
☆ What were their names? Where did they come from?
☆ What was their task or job?
☆ What are their stories?
Choose one person to create a profile about. Use the space below to take notes.

2. Create: Choose a creative way to present what you've learned about your person. You can
☆ write a short story from the person's perspective,
☆ create a poster or infographic,
☆ compose a song, or
☆ write a poem.

3. Present: Present your person's profile to your class.

....
....
....
....
....
....
....
....
....
....
....
....

From History to Stories

More creativity

★ Collaborative writing

You are to collect a "**journal** of the USA". The diary should include journaling or diary entries of people of different times and different cultures so that the **diversity** of U.S. history becomes **visible**. Decide which time periods you each want to write about. If necessary, do some research about the most important periods in U.S. history.

You can write stories from the perspectives of different groups like:
- ☆ Native Americans
- ☆ Asian Americans
- ☆ Hispanic or Latino Americans
- ☆ Black Americans
- ☆ Irish Americans

Remember: These definitions are mostly made up by white people and their labels might not **apply to** the stories and periods that, for example, Native Americans or Black Americans would consider most important.

---

1. Research: Do research on the specific time you choose. Decide from which point of view you want to write your diary entry: Should it be a famous person or some character you make up?

2. Write: Write the first **draft** of a diary entry. Talk about important events at the specific time, how your character finds out about them, what your character's everyday life looks like and feelings that they experience. Don't forget to note down a date.

3. Check: Read through your text again. Check spelling, grammar and punctuation. Add adjectives to make your text even more interesting to read.
Then, have a team member check your text and make comments on how you could improve your writing.

4. Write: Write down the final version of your diary entry. Use symbols, pictures and drawings to make your diary entry **livelier** and more **vivid**. Don't write and design more than one page.

5. Together: In your class, put the diary entries together in the order in which they happened.

6. Present and discuss: Talk about what you've learned through this project. What was easy to do for you? What was hard?

---

journal: das Tagebuch, **diversity:** die Vielfältigkeit, **visible:** sichtbar, **to apply to sth.:** sich auf etw. beziehen, **draft:** der Entwurf, **lively:** lebendig, **vivid:** anschaulich

Culture Kaleidoscope

What is this chapter about?

Die USA sind ein Land voller Unterschiede, verschiedener Kulturen und vielfältiger „icons". Amerikanische Ikonen und ihre Repräsentation in der Pop-Kultur bestimmen seit Jahrzehnten das Bild, das wir uns von dem Leben in den USA machen. Auch unsere Schüler*innen sind von der Kultur der USA geprägt und beeinflusst und bringen schon einiges (unbewusstes) Vorwissen mit. Es lohnt sich also, genauer mit unseren Lernenden hinzuschauen, was die Kultur(en) der USA eigentlich ausmacht. Was genau steckt dahinter? Welche Geschichten lassen sich hinter dem Sporthype und den großen Veranstaltungen rund um den Prom entdecken? Und was hat das mit unseren Lernenden ganz persönlich zu tun?

Dieses Kapitel möchte sich mit einigen exemplarischen „icons" der amerikanischen Kultur beschäftigen und damit einen kleinen Einblick in die Kultur der USA geben. Dafür erhalten Sie über jedes Thema ein Informationsblatt, welches knappes Überblickswissen liefert.

Im Anschluss an jedes „fact sheet" findet sich eine kreative Aufgabe, die die Schüler*innen dazu einlädt, die Informationen gestalterisch umzusetzen, sie mit ihrer eigenen Lebenswelt in Verbindung zu bringen oder sich noch intensiver damit auseinanderzusetzen. Die hier ausgewählten Themen reichen nicht, um der Diversität der USA in Gänze gerecht zu werden. Sie möchten jedoch einen ersten Eindruck geben und Lust darauf machen, das Land der unbegrenzten Möglichkeiten noch ein bisschen mehr zu entdecken.

Abb. © Yanina Nosova – Shutterstock.com

Culture Kaleidoscope

Team spirit!

Sports are extremely popular in the USA. Large numbers of people love to watch them on TV, at universities, colleges and high schools, or are active themselves. Sports were played by Native Americans to stay fit and healthy but also for ceremonial purposes and the early **settlers** also brought games with them that developed and became today's typical American sports: baseball, basketball and football. But watch out: "football" as played in England is called "soccer" in the USA and "American Football" is a completely different sport!

Being active and participating in different types of sports does not only keep you healthy: sports also play important social and political roles. Sports hold **communities** across the country together with local high school basketball games being the biggest event for the **residents** in many small towns. Fans of university teams get together in stadiums to **cheer** for their team and friends and families meet for parties in front of the TV when it comes to the Super Bowl. Also, sports **transmit values** such as **justice**, fair play and teamwork. They also play an important role when it comes to integration. Lots of young people only get the chance to attend college or go to university because of **scholarships** they **receive** for their outstanding performances in sports.

A nation's new pastime

During the last few years a new sport has become more and more popular in the USA: pickleball. It was invented in the 1960s on Bainbridge Island near Seattle when a few dads were trying to come up with a fun activity for their kids. It's a mix between badminton, tennis and table tennis with easy rules and is **suitable** for players of all ages and skills. The pickleball **court** is a lot smaller than a tennis court. This makes pickleball an extremely social sport: players can talk to each other during the game. But not everyone is a fan of pickleball: Neighbors across the country complain about the noise.

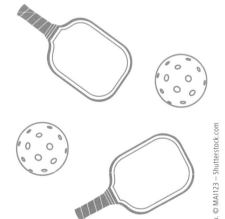

> **settler:** der Siedler/die Siedlerin, **community:** die Gemeinschaft, die Gemeinde, **resident:** der Bewohner/die Bewohnerin, **to cheer:** anfeuern, **to transmit:** vermitteln, **value:** der Wert, **justice:** die Gerechtigkeit, **scholarship:** das Stipendium, **to receive:** erhalten, **suitable:** geeignet, **court:** das Spielfeld

Culture Kaleidoscope

Team spirit!

⭐ Creating a jersey

1. Together: Get together in a team of three to four people.

2. Research: Find out about the most popular American sports. Which are their most popular teams? How do the teams represent the cities and regions that they are from? Try to divide the research tasks between all of you.

3. Create: In your group: Come up with your own fictional sports team. Which sport do they play? Where is it based? What name should your team have? (You don't have to stick to "real" sports but you can make up your own.)

Then, use the jersey template below to create your own design. Consider team colors, logos and symbols, numbers and additional graphics.

4. Present: Show your jersey to the class. Talk about the inspiration behind your design, the meaning behind the team colors, the name and the cultural elements that you included.

5. Discuss: Have your class vote for the best jersey. Which design is the most creative? Which is the most original?

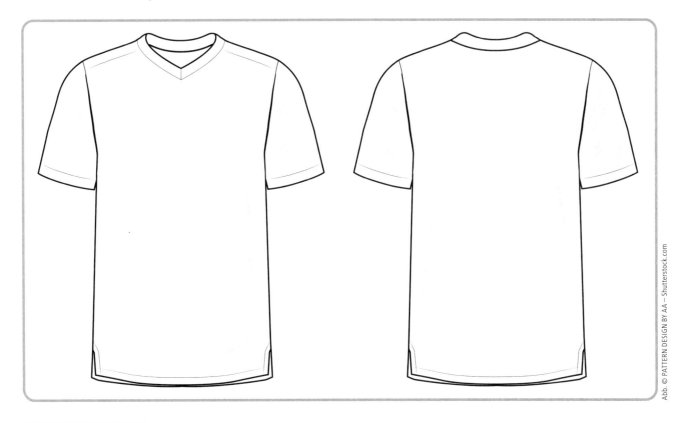

jersey: das Trikot

Culture Kaleidoscope

Let's celebrate!

With holidays all throughout the year, there is always a reason to celebrate. Most of the festivities do not have a religious meaning, but are rather meant to remember important historical events or people. Some of the celebrations, like Mardi Gras and Columbus Day can be **traced back** to diverse cultures, but nowadays they all have a typical "American **flavor**" to them.

Each state can make its own decision which holidays **are observed**. Most states agree to the same dates that the President **proclaims**, but it is a local decision whether people have to work on these days. Also schools might be closed on major holidays but not on some others.

> There are ten holidays that the **federal government** proclaims every year. Five of these holidays are celebrated on a Monday, the other five, like New Year's Day or Christmas Day are celebrated on a fixed date. If it happens to fall on a Sunday, usually the following Monday is also a holiday.
> The ten federal holidays are: New Year's Day, Martin Luther King Day, Presidents' Day, Memorial Day, Independence Day, Labor Day, Columbus Day, Veterans Day, Thanksgiving Day, Christmas Day.

Independence Day

Happy birthday, USA! When the USA became a free and **independent** nation, it was time to celebrate – and it still is today. Independence Day is also called the "Fourth of July". This is the date on which the Declaration of Independence was agreed on: July 4, 1776. It's a day of national patriotic celebrations with shows, games, **bonfires**, fireworks and parades. Often families meet to celebrate together.

> **to trace back:** zurückverfolgen, **flavor:** (*wörtlich*) der Geschmack, **to observe sth.:** etw. begehen, **to proclaim sth.:** etw. verkünden, **federal government:** die Staatsregierung, **independent:** unabhängig, **bonfire:** das Lagerfeuer

Culture Kaleidoscope

Let's celebrate!

⭐ Designing a parade float

A lot of parades are held on the Fourth of July throughout the country. They often feature colorful **floats** and bands.

1. Research: Find out more about parades held on Independence Day. What makes them special? Which elements are common?

2. Think: Which elements would you include in a float to **commemorate** Independence Day? Decide on one topic for your float, for example: historic or recent events, patriotic symbols or important people.

3. Create: Use a blank sheet of paper to draw on. Use colored pencils and pens to design and decorate your parade float. Add details, colors and decorations to reflect your theme.

Label key elements of your float design. Give short descriptions or write **captions**.

4. Present: Show your float design to your class. Explain your theme, your key elements and the creative features.

5. Discuss: Talk about Independence Day parades in your class. Share your thoughts on what you think is interesting or exciting about them. Also talk about whether Germany has a similar tradition of parades.

6. Reflect: Have each class member say two sentences. What have you learned during this project? How did you feel designing your float?

> **float:** der Umzugswagen, **to commemorate sth.**: an etw. erinnern, **caption:** die Bildunterschrift

Culture Kaleidoscope

High school stories

U.S. school bus

Have you ever wondered if the U.S. school system would **suit** you? You might have seen a couple of movies about school life in the USA and noticed that it is very different from school life in Germany.

 Schools in the U.S. typically have 12 **grade** levels, starting from kindergarten and going on to 12th grade. After graduating high school, students usually go to college or start working. There is no **curriculum** that all schools have to follow but students usually take tests at the end of high school, like the SAT or ACT, which they need for their college **admission**.

The world of American teens

The typical school day starts in the morning and ends in the afternoon. Iconic yellow buses take students to and from school. Students study different subjects including English, math, **science** and **social studies**. They also have **elective** classes like art, music and foreign languages. Schools offer lunches in their cafeterias and the afternoons are filled with classes and **extracurricular** activities, like band practice, **drama group**, sports or club meetings. At the end of the day, students throw their stuff in their **lockers** and head on home.

Could you imagine your whole life taking place at school? You'd go there with all people of your area, you'd have all your friends there, most of your hobbies would take place at school and you'd probably find your first love there. And then during the end of your time at school, there would be the highlight of your school life: PROM! It's a formal dance at the end of the school year. Students ask each other out on dates, wear fancy dresses and **tuxedos**. It's a major step on the way of becoming a grown-up and students spend months planning this special night.

> **to suit sth./sb.:** passend sein für etw./jmd., **grade:** die Jahrgangsstufe, **curriculum:** der Lehrplan, **admission:** die Zulassung, **science:** die Naturwissenschaft, **social studies:** Sozialkunde, **elective:** Wahl-, **extracurricular:** außerhalb des Lehrplans, **drama group:** die Theatergruppe, **locker:** der Spind, das Schließfach, **tuxedo:** der Smoking

Culture Kaleidoscope

High school stories

⭐ Planning a prom night

1. Together: Get together in groups of three to four people. You will come up with the plan for a prom night at the end of your school year.

2. Brainstorm: Come up with ideas for your prom night. These questions can help you:
- ☆ Which theme should it have?
- ☆ Will there be a special color range to use?
- ☆ What kind of decorations are needed?
- ☆ Which kind of music do you choose? Will there be a band, a DJ or will you just use a playlist?
- ☆ What special activities will there be?

Note down your ideas in the mind map below. Use symbols and colored pencils to make your ideas stand out.

3. Create: Use a blank sheet of paper to create an invitation or a poster for your prom night. Remember to include important details like date and time, dress code and other relevant information.

4. Present: Share your ideas and your invitation or poster with your class.

5. Discuss: Talk about what makes a good prom night.

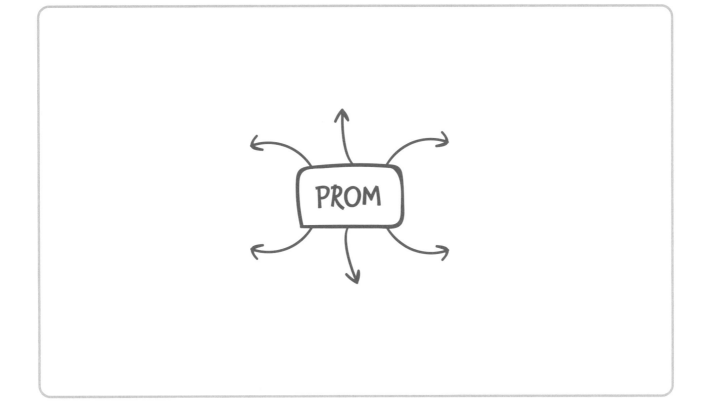

Culture Kaleidoscope

Harmonizing with the stars

The USA is a diverse country which can also be seen in the wide variety of music genres. Lots of them were created in the U.S. and have spread across the globe. Jazz, for example, **originated** in New Orleans and is seen as "America's classical music". Blues has its **roots** deep in the African American culture, as has gospel. Rock'n'Roll appeared in the 1950s and revolutionized the world of music. Country music reflects the life and stories of people in the areas far from the big cities. In the 1970s, another genre came up which has had a huge impact on global pop culture with is beats and powerful lyrics: hip hop. And pop music has produced **countless** stars that are popular all over the world.

 Music has always played a big role in social and political activism. American music is a **melting pot** of different cultures, with artists from different backgrounds. Their **fame** often gives a voice to people who often don't get heard in **society**.

Music culture

From the blues bars in Chicago to the jazz clubs in New Orleans, from music festivals like Coachella to the Grammy Awards: music plays an important role in American culture. Music is an important part of entertainment. People go to concerts, festivals and to clubs. Additionally, music is a fundamental part of celebrations and festivals: for example, the fireworks at July 4 come with patriotic songs and the Mardi Gras parades with jazz bands. Moreover, schools offer music education programs giving students the chance to **explore** their own musical talents, get creative and **promote cultural awareness** – also: it's a lot of fun!

Alle Abb. © lemono – Shutterstock.com

---

to originate: entstehen, **root:** die Wurzel, **countless:** unzählig, **melting pot:** der Schmelztiegel, **fame:** der Ruhm, die Bekanntheit, **society:** die Gesellschaft, **to explore sth.:** etw. erkunden, **to promote:** voranbringen, unterstützen, **cultural awareness:** das kulturelle Bewusstsein

Culture Kaleidoscope

Harmonizing with the stars

⭐ Creating a star portrait

1. Research: Research an American music star. It can be someone who is still alive or someone who had a big impact in the past. It could be a singer, guitarist, drummer, rapper etc. Find out detailed information about this person. Include information like their music, the lyrics, and their achievements (in- and outside of the musical world).

2. Write: Write a short song text about your star. Remember to include at least three verses and a chorus. Use the section below to take notes.

3. Create: Use a blank sheet of paper to put together a collage about your star. You could also draw a portrait of them. Remember to add your lyrics as well as symbols that support the information you're giving.

4. Present: Pick a short snippet of a song by your artist that you can use in your presentation. Talk about your star portrait in front of your class. Give them the most important information. Present them the snippet and tell them why you like this part of the song so much.

5. Discuss: Put up all portraits around the classroom. Have everyone walk round and look at the works.
Talk about the different music stars in class. Discuss if there were any new pieces of information that you've learned and what you think was most interesting.
Also talk about if and why (not) music plays an important role in your life and what kind of music you like to listen to most.

....

....

....

....

....

....

....

....

Reflexionsimpulse

Warum Reflexion?

Reflexionsfragen am Ende einer Lerneinheit tragen dazu bei, das eigene Handeln genauer zu betrachten und so Erkenntnisse für die Zukunft zu gewinnen. Sie helfen dabei, Kompetenzen aufzubauen, die lebenslanges selbstgesteuertes Lernen ermöglichen. Reflexionsfragen lassen sich dabei in zwei große Kategorien einteilen: prozessorientierte und produktorientierte Reflexion. Beide Kategorien sind für das Lernen des Lernens wichtig. Gleichzeitig gibt es auch Fragen, die sich je nach Kontext für beide Arten der Reflexion einsetzen lassen.

Die Fragen werden am Ende einer Einheit gestellt. Dabei ist es je nach Setting und Lerngruppe möglich, mit einzelnen Lernenden zu sprechen, die Reflexion in Kleingruppen oder auch in der ganzen Klasse durchzuführen.

Für den fremdsprachlichen Unterricht bieten sich vorgegebene Satzanfänge oft besser an als Fragen. Dies dient der Verständlichkeit und ist für die Schüler*innen mitunter deutlich leichter umzusetzen.

Wie funktioniert's?

Bei allem Wissen um die Notwendigkeit guter Lernreflexion: Eine Reflexion kostet Zeit – ein Gut, das wir im Unterrichtsalltag oft nicht genügend zur Verfügung haben. Eine einfache und schnelle Art der Reflexion bietet ein Blitzlicht/round robin, bei dem alle die Gelegenheit haben, diese beiden Satzanfänge kurz und knackig mit eigenen Erkenntnissen zu ergänzen:

☆ What went well: Die Schüler*innen nennen Dinge, die gut liefen.
☆ Even better if: Die Schüler*innen nennen, was sie zum Verbessern ihrer Arbeit benötigen.

Auf den nächsten Seiten finden sich Satzanfänge, die sich in der Unterrichtspraxis bewährt haben. Ich habe mich bemüht, ein möglichst universelles Set aus 14 Fragen zusammenzustellen, die ein breites Spektrum an Reflexion ermöglichen. Manche der Fragen sind klar prozess-, andere klar produktorientiert. Andere lassen sich in beide Richtungen füllen und sind so noch vielfältiger einsetzbar – bedürfen damit aber eventuell auch mehr Steuerung, um echte Erkenntnisse zu gewinnen.

Alle (oder ausgewählte) Satzanfänge werden präsentiert. Dies kann anhand einlaminierter Karten in der Mitte eines Sitzkreises oder durch die Visualisierung an der Tafel oder Wand geschehen. Alle Schüler*innen kommen reihum zu Wort. Dabei wird ein Satzanfang gewählt und der Satz vervollständigt.

Anhang

Impulsfragen-Katalog

Prozessorientierte Fragen:
- ☆ We worked well in our team because … .
- ☆ I had trouble with … .
- ☆ Next time I would do … in a different way because … .
- ☆ Next time it would be even better to … .

Produktorientierte Fragen:
- ☆ Something new that I learned is … .
- ☆ I am happy with the result because … .
- ☆ The result would be even better if … .
- ☆ One thing that I still don't understand is … .

Weiterführende Reflexionsfragen:
- ☆ I am proud of … .
- ☆ I want to praise … because. … .
- ☆ One thing that surprised me was … .
- ☆ I want to find out even more about … .
- ☆ I really enjoyed … .
- ☆ One thing that I discovered about my learning is … .

Wichtig! Die folgenden Regeln müssen klar sein:
- ☆ Alle dürfen ihre Eindrücke frei schildern.
- ☆ Es gibt keine negativen Reaktionen oder Kommentare.
- ☆ Wertschätzende und interessierte Rückfragen sind aber durchaus möglich.

Und nun viel Freude beim Erkenntnisgewinn!

Lösungen

 The USA – Scavenger Hunt (S. 25–26):

Question 1: Alaska

Question 2: New York

Question 3: Pennsylvania

Question 4: Michigan

Question 5: North Carolina

Question 6: Florida

Question 7: Illinois

Question 8: Arizona

Question 9: California

Question 10: South Dakota

Question 11: Texas

Question 12: Wyoming

Solution sentence: That was a piece of cake!

Meaning: When you say that something was "a piece of cake", it means that the thing was something that isn't hard to do.

When your friend asks you how the test was and you answer, "It was a piece of cake!", you're saying that it was very easy.

Similar ways to express that something was easy or not hard to do are: "Easy peasy!" or "It was a walk in the park!"